Biomedical
Ethics

Current Issues

ReferencePoint
Press®

San Diego, CA

Other books in the Compact Research Current Issues set:

*For a complete list of titles please visit www.referencepointpress.com.

Biomedical Ethics

Andrea C. Nakaya

Current Issues

ReferencePoint
Press®

San Diego, CA

© 2012 ReferencePoint Press, Inc.
Printed in the United States

For more information, contact:
ReferencePoint Press, Inc.
PO Box 27779
San Diego, CA 92198
www.ReferencePointPress.com

Picture credits:
Cover: Dreamstime and iStockphoto.com
Maury Aaseng: 32–35, 46–49, 60–62, 75–77
Dr. Yorgos Nikas/Science Photo Library: 15
Saturn Stills/Science Photo Library: 11

LIBRARY OF CONGRESS CATALOGING-IN-PUBLICATION DATA

Nakaya, Andrea C., 1976–
   Biomedical ethics / by Andrea C. Nakaya.
      p. cm. — (Compact research series)
   Includes bibliographical references and index.
   ISBN-13: 978-1-60152-157-6 (hardback)
   ISBN-10: 1-60152-157-X (hardback)
   1. Medical ethics—Juvenile literature. 2. Bioethics—Juvenile literature. I. Title.
   R724.N347   2012
   174.2—dc23
                                                                                    2011019042

Contents

Foreword

66**Where is the knowledge we have lost in information?**99

—T.S. Eliot, "The Rock."

As modern civilization continues to evolve, its ability to create, store, distribute, and access information expands exponentially. The explosion of information from all media continues to increase at a phenomenal rate. By 2020 some experts predict the worldwide information base will double every 73 days. While access to diverse sources of information and perspectives is paramount to any democratic society, information alone cannot help people gain knowledge and understanding. Information must be organized and presented clearly and succinctly in order to be understood. The challenge in the digital age becomes not the creation of information, but how best to sort, organize, enhance, and present information.

ReferencePoint Press developed the *Compact Research* series with this challenge of the information age in mind. More than any other subject area today, researching current issues can yield vast, diverse, and unqualified information that can be intimidating and overwhelming for even the most advanced and motivated researcher. The *Compact Research* series offers a compact, relevant, intelligent, and conveniently organized collection of information covering a variety of current topics ranging from illegal immigration and deforestation to diseases such as anorexia and meningitis.

The series focuses on three types of information: objective single-author narratives, opinion-based primary source quotations, and facts and statistics. The clearly written objective narratives provide context and reliable background information. Primary source quotes are carefully selected and cited, exposing the reader to differing points of view. And facts and statistics sections aid the reader in evaluating perspectives. Presenting these key types of information creates a richer, more balanced learning experience.

For better understanding and convenience, the series enhances information by organizing it into narrower topics and adding design features that make it easy for a reader to identify desired content. For example, in *Compact Research: Illegal Immigration*, a chapter covering the economic impact of illegal immigration has an objective narrative explaining the various ways the economy is impacted, a balanced section of numerous primary source quotes on the topic, followed by facts and full-color illustrations to encourage evaluation of contrasting perspectives.

The ancient Roman philosopher Lucius Annaeus Seneca wrote, "It is quality rather than quantity that matters." More than just a collection of content, the *Compact Research* series is simply committed to creating, finding, organizing, and presenting the most relevant and appropriate amount of information on a current topic in a user-friendly style that invites, intrigues, and fosters understanding.

Biomedical Ethics at a Glance

A Continuously Changing Field
Rapid changes in medical technology give rise to many new ethical issues—issues that bioethicists debate but cannot always resolve.

Genetic Testing
Genetic testing now allows people to learn about their chances of developing hundreds of different genetic diseases but raises questions about discrimination, reliability of test results, and with whom the results should be shared.

Embryo Screening
Through genetic screening of embryos parents can select for sex or prevent the birth of children with devastating diseases such as Tay-Sachs, but critics charge that such testing objectifies children and discriminates against the disabled.

Potential of Embryonic Stem Cell Research
Embryonic stem cell research has the potential to cure many illnesses, but it raises questions about whether destroying an embryo for this purpose is ethical and whether this research should be federally funded.

Alternatives to Embryonic Stem Cells
Other types of stem cells offer an alternative to embryonic stem cell research, but critics say that embryonic stem cells hold the most promise for curing many diseases.

Assisted Reproductive Technology

Assisted reproductive technology expands the range of people who can have children but has raised ethical questions about health risks, the structure of the family, and unequal access to this technology.

Surrogacy in India

Because surrogacy services are cheaper and legally simpler in India, many people from many different countries now travel to India for such services. While some people believe this gives Indian women a chance to improve their lives, others contend that it exploits them.

Physician-Assisted Suicide

Physician-assisted suicide is legal only in Oregon and Washington; however, people in all states continue to debate the ethics of legalization.

Potential for Abuse

People disagree about the results of legalizing physician-assisted suicide; advocates insist that little abuse occurs in places where it is legal, while opponents contend that widespread abuse occurs but is not reported.

Overview

❝It would be difficult to imagine moral issues more important . . . than those addressed by bioethics.❞

—Lewis Vaughn, bioethicist.

❝It is unclear what the field of bioethics can add in the way of unique scholarship, practical wisdom, or ethical reflection that is not already being applied today . . . by experts in [other fields].❞

—Sally Satel, psychiatrist.

During World War II the Nazis conducted medical experiments on large numbers of prisoners in concentration camps. Unwilling participants were left disfigured, disabled, or dead as the result of experiments that included freezing, burning, and poisoning them. When these actions were later revealed, many of the doctors involved insisted that no international law prevented such experimentation. As a result of such atrocities, some people started to study the ethics of medicine in an effort to develop principles and standards to guide conduct in the field. This led to the emergence of the discipline of bioethics in the 1960s, and in the United States today hundreds of bioethics organizations are studying a growing number of biomedical ethics topics.

What Is Biomedical Ethics?

Biomedical ethics is the study of ethical issues in medicine and biology. Using the methods of philosophy, bioethicists try to discover what

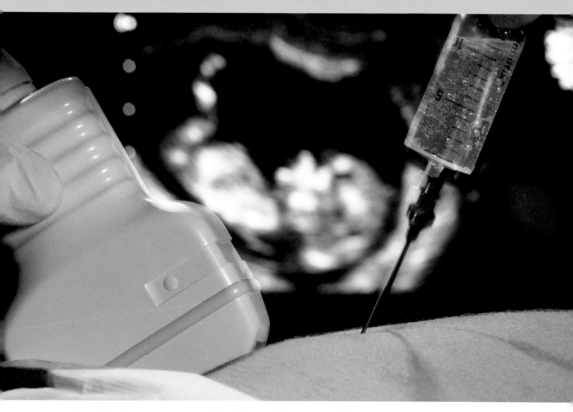

A needle draws amniotic fluid from the uterus of a pregnant woman. The cells in the extracted fluid will be screened for genetic or chromosomal disorders such as Down syndrome. Tests such as this can provide valuable information but can also raise ethical questions.

is right and wrong and what moral standards should guide conduct in these fields. As medical technology changes, new ethical issues continue to arise, so bioethicists constantly face new questions. For example, advances in reproductive technology now allow parents to screen embryos to select the sex of their baby. Bioethicists explore the ethical implications of this technology and whether it is ethical to destroy the excess embryos that are created in the process. Medicine and biology are changing rapidly and constantly, and bioethicists believe they have an important role in examining the implications of such changes. Explain bioethics scholars Robert M. Veatch, Amy M. Haddad, and Dan C. English, "We are living in the era of the biological revolution. . . . Medicine is remaking humans. At the same time, it is posing problems to be pondered by patients and professionals alike."[1]

Bioethicists work in a variety of places, including schools, hospitals, and in government offices, where they offer guidance about ethical issues. Many universities have bioethics centers that offer numerous bioethics programs to students. Bioethicists are even involved in the highest level of US government; in 2009 President Barack Obama created the Presidential Commission for the Study of Bioethical Issues to advise him.

Beneficence and Nonmaleficence

Beneficence and nonmaleficence are two important moral principles in biomedical ethics that address the obligations of health care professionals to those in their care. Nonmaleficence is the obligation not to cause injury or harm to one's patients. An example of a nonmaleficent action is to stop a person from taking a medication that is shown to be harmful to him or her. However, in medicine, situations often arise in which medical treatments do risk harm to patients—for example, chemotherapy treatment for cancer—and the health care provider's responsibility in such cases is to make sure the benefits outweigh the risks. To help them make difficult decisions such as whether to prescribe chemotherapy, medical professionals use the principle of beneficence, the obligation to act in the best interest of patients and to place their well-being first.

> " In the United States today hundreds of bioethics organizations are studying a growing number of biomedical ethics topics. "

While it is widely agreed that beneficence and nonmaleficence are important principles that should guide bioethics, how to follow these principles is often disputed. This is because there is no universal agreement about how best to prevent harm and facilitate well-being. In addition, actions that prevent harm and facilitate well-being for one person may have a different impact on others. For example, a terminally ill person may believe death is in his or her best interest and request help from a doctor in dying. However assisted suicide also affects the doctor who performs the act and the family of the terminally ill person, and preventing harm and facilitating well-being means considering the effect of assisted suicide on all these people.

The Doctor-Patient Relationship

Many bioethical issues involve questions about the relationship between doctor and patient. Ethical conflicts are often between the right of the patient to make his or her own decisions and the obligation of the doctor to do what is best for the patient. Three important concepts that arise in these conflicts are autonomy, informed consent, and paternalism.

Autonomy is a person's power to freely deliberate the available options and to choose one. Informed consent is an important part of autonomy. In order to make a choice, patients first need to discuss different treatment options with the health care provider and make a decision about treatment. Medical professionals should adequately disclose all the information needed to make the decision, and the patient must have the ability to understand all this information.

> "As medical technology changes, new ethical issues continue to arise."

Autonomy becomes complicated when a patient's desire for personal freedom conflicts with a doctor's duty to help the patient. When doctors decide on their own what is best for their patients, this is called paternalism. Bioethicist Lewis Vaughn defines paternalism as "the overriding of a person's actions or decision-making for his own good." Vaughn explains that the social importance given to autonomy versus paternalism has changed over time. He says, "Early medical practice was strongly paternalistic." But, says Vaughn, "Over the last few decades . . . society has placed more value on the rights of patients to know important facts regarding their medical care, to make choices regarding their medical treatment, and even to refuse treatment that physicians recommend."[2]

Can Genetic Testing and Manipulation Be Done Ethically?

Genes are a code that exists in every human cell and holds all the information that decides how a human body is made. Whether people will have blue eyes or brown eyes, whether their blood type will be A or B, and even their chance of developing breast cancer or Alzheimer's disease are all found in the genes. Researchers continue to expand their understanding of this genetic code. With increased understanding comes the ability to test a person for various genetic traits and diseases. Researchers now have the ability to test embryos for numerous genetic diseases such as Down syndrome and even some physical traits such as sex. Adults can also undergo genetic testing, which can reveal the presence, or likelihood of developing, a large number of genetic disorders. In addition to simply testing for such disorders, researchers are now trying to eliminate some of them by manipulating the genes through gene therapy.

> **Bioethicists work in a variety of places, including schools, hospitals, and in government offices.**

However, all this genetic testing and manipulation raises many ethical questions. Some people believe so much power to know the future or to alter oneself or one's children is unethical and that society should accept each human being for the unique combination of genes that he or she is. Others contend that using genetic testing and manipulation to improve society is logical and inevitable. Says ethicist Ronald M. Green, "Why should we think that the human genome is a once-and-for-all-finished, untamperable product? All of the biblically derived faiths permit human beings to improve on nature using technology, from agriculture to aviation. Why not improve our genome?"[3]

Is the Use of Human Embryos in Stem Cell Research Ethical?

Human embryonic stem cells (hESC) are cells taken from an early-stage embryo that is about five days old. They are different from any other type of cell in the human body because they are undifferentiated. This means that unlike all other cells, they do not yet have any specialized function, such as heart cells, or skin cells. They are also pluripotent, meaning that they have the ability to turn into any kind of specialized cell.

Researchers believe that embryonic stem cells have great potential to help them understand and cure many devastating diseases. The National Institutes of Health explains:

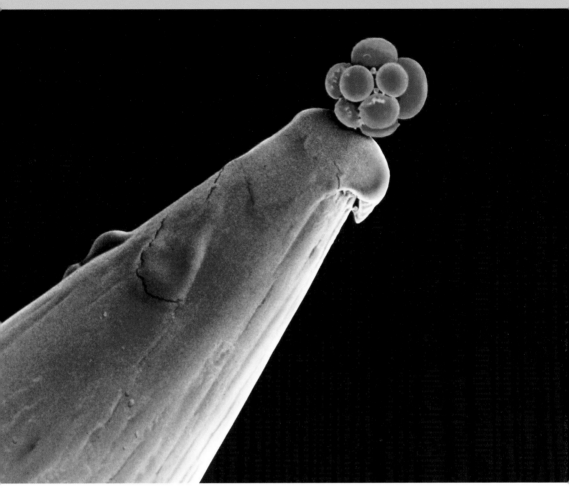

An early-stage human embryo is seen on the tip of a pin through a colored scanning electron micrograph. The cells will multiply to form the blastocyst. Stem cells taken from the blastocyst have the ability to turn into all types of specialized cells but their removal leads to ethical questions because the process destroys the embryo.

Studying stem cells will help us understand how they transform into the dazzling array of specialized cells that make us what we are. Some of the most serious medical conditions, such as cancer and birth defects, are due to problems that occur somewhere in this process. A better understanding of normal cell development will allow us to understand and perhaps correct the errors that cause these medical conditions.[4]

In addition, says the NIH, embryonic stem cells have great potential to make cells and tissues for transplantation. It says, "Stem cells offer the possibility of a renewable source of replacement cells and tissues to treat a myriad of diseases, conditions, and disabilities including Parkinson's disease, . . . spinal cord injury, burns, heart disease, diabetes, and arthritis."[5]

However, taking stem cells from an embryo also means the destruction of the embryo, so embryonic stem cell research has many critics. Opponents insist that no matter how small it is, an embryo is a human life, and its destruction is unethical, regardless of the potential benefits.

Is Assisted Reproductive Technology Ethical?

Many people who want to have children cannot because of infertility or some other biological reason. Assisted reproductive technology (ART) has developed to help these people by assisting the beginning of new human life in a laboratory. Doctors can use eggs and sperm from either parents or donors and fertilize an egg in the laboratory, then implant it in a woman's uterus. They can even freeze embryos and sperm to use later. The most common type of assisted reproductive technology in the United States is in vitro fertilization (IVF), in which an egg and sperm are combined outside the body and the resulting embryo is then transferred to woman's uterus. The first successful birth from in vitro fertilization took place in 1978.

Continuing advances in assisted reproductive technologies allow more and more people to have biologically related children; however, new technology also raises new ethical questions. Says Vaughn, "At every turn, [assisted reproductive technologies] generate ethical questions and serious debate about the nature and meaning of the family, the welfare of children, the treatment of women, the moral status of embryos, the value of human life, the sanctity of natural procreation, and the legitimacy of reproductive rights."[6]

Should Doctors Be Allowed to Help Patients Die?

One of the oldest issues debated in the field of biomedical ethics is whether doctors should be allowed to help patients die. People may have many different reasons for wanting help in ending their lives, but the debate about assisted suicide usually centers on those people who have a terminal illness. Some terminally ill people are in great pain or believe that their quality of life is so poor that it is not worth living, so they want a doctor's help in dying. Proponents believe that such people have a right to choose to end their pain and suffering. Critics contend that people should not have the power to end lives. They believe that legalizing assisted suicide would harm the relationship between doctor and patient and might lead to abuses such as the assisted suicide of children or the mentally incompetent. Assisted suicide is legal only in a few places in the world, and the topic continues to be intensely debated.

Synthetic Biology

Synthetic biology is an emerging field in which researchers design and construct biological parts and systems that are not found in nature. In May 2010 researchers at the J. Craig Venter Institute announced a major breakthrough in synthetic biology, with the creation of the first self-replicating synthetic bacteria. Advocates believe that synthetic biology has the potential to benefit people in many ways, such as creating new medicines and vaccines and increasing researchers' understanding of many complex biological processes.

Yet critics are concerned about numerous ethical questions. A major concern is the accidental or intentional release of a harmful synthetic molecule or organism outside the controlled research setting. Critics also question whether it is ethical for humans to have the power to create new organisms. Finally, they worry about questions of fairness and equality that may arise with such powerful new technology, including who should control it and who should have access to it.

> **Many bioethical issues involve questions about the relationship between doctor and patient.**

The Presidential Commission for the Study of Bioethical Issues, created to advise the president, suggests caution in this field:

> It [is] imprudent either to declare a moratorium on synthetic biology until all risks can be determined and mitigated, or to simply 'let science rip,' regardless of the likely risks. . . . The Commission instead proposes a middle ground—an ongoing system of *prudent vigilance* that carefully monitors, identifies, and mitigates potential and realized harms over time.[7]

Human Subjects Research

Human subjects research, in which people are observed for the purpose of research, is essential to many medical advances. Explain bioethicists Thomas A. Shannon and Nicholas J. Kockler, "Probably no feature of modern medicine has had as dramatic an effect on so many people as research. By careful design and countless hours of running experiments, scientists have succeeded in identifying the causes of many diseases, designing vaccines to prevent them, and developing drugs and devices to treat them."[8]

However, the use of people for research raises ethical issues, such as how much to inform them about the research being conducted and how to protect them from harm. A famous example illustrating the importance of ethical standards for human subjects research is the Tuskegee syphilis study. Between 1932 and 1972 doctors in Tuskegee, Alabama, allowed 400 poor and mostly illiterate African American men to live with untreated syphilis in order to study the natural effects of the disease. Some men died, wives contracted the disease, and children were born with congenital syphilis. Tuskegee University says, "The Tuskegee Syphilis Study is one of the most horrendous examples of research carried out in disregard of basic ethical principles of conduct."[9]

> " **Genetic testing and manipulation raises many ethical questions.** "

In 1974, following revelations of the Tuskegee study, the National Commission for the Protection of Human Subjects of Biomedical and Behavioral Research was created. The commission's 1979 *Belmont Report: Ethical Principles and Guidelines for the Protection of Human Subjects Research* explains the fundamental ethical principles that should be used for human subjects research. This report continues to be an important guide for human subjects research in the United States.

The Ethics of Organ Donation

Organ donation is an ethical issue that affects thousands of lives every year in the United States. Many people need donated organs to replace their own failing ones. The United Network for Organ Sharing manages the nation's organ transplant system under contract with the federal government. It states that in March 2011 more than 110,000 people were waiting for transplants of organs such as hearts, lungs, and livers. This demand greatly exceeds supply, and people on the waiting list die every day.

> **One of the oldest issues debated in the field of biomedical ethics is whether doctors should be allowed to help patients die.**

As a result of the organ shortage, ethicists debate how organs should be obtained for donation. In the United States a deceased person's organs can be taken only if he or she has previously and explicitly consented to donation by filling out a donor card or checking a box on his or her driver's license. However, many people are critical of this policy because they believe it unnecessarily reduces the number of donations made. Explains bioethicist Arthur Caplan,

> Numerous polls and surveys show that most Americans are willing to be organ donors upon their deaths. Yet the system we have in place now—using donor cards and driver's license check-offs—to permit people to let their wishes be known does not capture the altruism and goodwill that is out there. Cards and licenses get lost or misplaced or those who sign them fail to talk about their wishes with their families meaning that organs are buried or cremated when they could be saving lives.[10]

Some people argue that a policy of presumed consent would be more beneficial. Such a policy presumes that a person is an organ donor unless he or she indicates otherwise. Austria, Norway, and some other countries follow this policy. However, critics charge that this policy is unethical because a person has not explicitly agreed and may not have been informed about all the implications of donation.

Technology Advances Mean More Ethical Questions

In a world where researchers and doctors are continually increasing their ability to understand and manipulate human life, biomedical ethics is a vitally important discipline that involves increasingly complicated questions. As the Presidential Commission for the Study of Bioethical Issues explains, while new technology can greatly improve life, it is important to consider all its implications, including the possible negative ones. The commission cautions, "The mere fact that something new can be done does not mean that it ought to be done. The history of science here and abroad is sadly full of examples of intellectual freedom exercised without responsibility that resulted in appalling affronts to vulnerable populations, the environment, and the ideals of the profession of science itself."[11]

Bioethicists serve as a check against such possible harms by educating society about the ethical implications of new technology. As Shannon and Kockler explain, while members of society may disagree on various technologies, biomedical ethics is something that everybody should think about. They warn: "We need to be informed citizens [in regard to bioethics] if for no reason than that the developments in these fields have a profound impact on our lives and our society."[12]

Can Genetic Testing and Manipulation Be Done Ethically?

> **Genetic testing is a revolutionary way to protect yourself and the ones you love from unknowns and potential future illnesses.**
>
> —Anna Peterson, graduate student who submitted a DNA sample for at-home genetic testing.

> **[With genetic testing] we now have a range of choices that we never had before. These choices are frequently problematic.**
>
> —Thomas A. Shannon and Nicholas J. Kockler, bioethicists.

In 2008 first lady of Iceland Dorrit Moussaieff submitted a sample of her DNA to a testing company to better understand her genetic makeup. Researchers' analysis of her DNA included the following: Moussaieff has a very small chance of developing Alzheimer's disease, an average risk of becoming obese, a higher-than-average risk of stroke, and a genetic tendency toward developing lactose intolerance. This is just one example of the many types of genetic testing that researchers are now capable of. Yet along with increasing abilities for genetic testing and manipulation comes great ethical controversy.

Preimplantation genetic diagnosis (PGD) is a genetic test done in conjunction with in vitro fertilization, a process by which egg cells are fertilized by sperm in a laboratory and then implanted in the uterus.

With preimplantation genetic diagnosis, doctors create multiple embryos in the laboratory, then test them for chromosomal abnormalities, disease-related genes, or even sex, and choose the desirable embryos for transfer. This technique was developed to allow couples at risk of passing on a serious genetic disease such as Tay-Sachs disease or cystic fibrosis to have children who would not be affected by such diseases. Many people agree that it is desirable to prevent serious diseases such as Tay-Sachs, in which nerve cells are rapidly destroyed and a child becomes blind, deaf, unable to swallow, and paralyzed and usually dies by age four. Critiques of genetic screening usually focus on its use to prevent less serious genetic disorders and to select traits such as sex. Opponents worry that genetic screening encourages society to view children as manufactured objects rather than unique gifts. They also charge that using the test to eliminate genetic disorders is discriminatory to people who have these disorders.

> **Along with increasing abilities for genetic testing and manipulation comes great ethical controversy.**

A controversial use of genetic screening is to create "savior siblings," siblings who will have matching tissues to donate to an existing sick child. The first reported case of this happened in Colorado when Molly Nash, born in 1994, was diagnosed with Fanconi anemia, a genetic disease that is usually fatal. Her only hope for survival was a blood and marrow transplant. However, the transplant was unlikely to succeed unless it came from a sibling who had an exact blood match. Molly's parents used the test to have another child who was a match. After her brother Adam was born, Molly received his cord blood, and today both children are in good health. However, this case and many subsequent ones have resulted in intense controversy over whether it is ethical to create a savior sibling. Critics worry about the effects on the savior child, the sick child, and family dynamics. There is also concern that parents might approve invasive procedures to obtain transplant tissues from their savior child.

Many disabled people and advocates for the rights of the disabled are opposed to preimplantation genetic diagnosis and embryo screening because they feel it is discriminatory and reduces diversity. Critics point out that when people use genetic testing to avoid having a child with disabilities, they are sending the message that a disabled person is better off not born. Yet many people with disabilities have lives that are rewarding and meaningful to them and to those around them.

Critics also argue that in addition to being prejudicial to people with certain genetic conditions and disabilities, increased genetic screening is reducing the number of babies born with these conditions and thus reducing diversity in society. Bioethicist Arthur Caplan points out that this can have many implications for members of society, including less support for people who do have genetic diseases and disabilities. He says, "As some

> **Opponents worry that genetic screening encourages society to view children as manufactured objects rather than unique gifts.**

families with a Down syndrome child have noted, fewer kids with Down may mean fewer public programs, fewer resources in schools and for housing and less political clout. If some genetic diseases begin to fade away, will society's willingness to provide support for the diminishing numbers of those born with such diseases fade as well?"[13]

Implications of Test Results

In the past, few people knew they had a genetic disease such as Huntington's until they began to experience symptoms. Today, however, researchers are able to identify many disease-related genes. Before any symptoms appear they can test a person for the presence of numerous genetic diseases or the likelihood of developing many illnesses such as breast cancer or Alzheimer's disease. Some people do not want such knowledge because in most cases no treatment is yet available for these diseases. However, others welcome the opportunity to be prepared for possible health problems or to avoid passing them on to their children.

After a genetic test has been done, the individual tested and his or her health care providers may face difficulties in deciding to whom they should reveal the test results. As genetic technology expert Doris Teichler Zallen points out, genetic testing may affect more than just the individual tested. She explains, "Genes are shared in families. A genetic test that provides information about one person can, at the same time, indicate to others in the family that they too may have the same gene. More than any other type of testing, a genetic test of a single individual is actually a test of a whole family."[14] Some people believe they have a moral obligation to share test results with other relatives who might also be affected and want to prepare themselves for future health problems or avoid passing along genetic disorders through their own children. Others decide not to share results because they do not want to be stigmatized for possessing flawed genes.

At-Home Genetic Testing

Until recently, if a person wanted to undergo genetic testing, he or she had to go to a health care provider who would do the test and interpret the results. Now, however, consumers can purchase at-home genetic tests over the Internet or by phone. In at-home genetic testing the consumer collects a DNA sample at home, often a saliva sample, and mails it back to the laboratory. The person is notified of the results by mail, phone, or online. The price ranges from a hundred to thousands of dollars. Sometimes a genetic counselor or health care provider is available to answer questions, but at-home genetic tests do not necessarily involve a health care provider.

> **When people use genetic testing to avoid having a child with disabilities, they are sending the message that a disabled person is better off not born.**

Advocates of at-home tests maintain that they are a good way for individuals to obtain genetic information about themselves while ensuring privacy. One company that offers direct-to-consumer genetic testing says, "People have the right to access their personal genetic information. Genetic information is a fundamental element of a person's body, identity and individuality. . . . We believe our customers are capable of understanding the context of the information we provide them. We also think the benefits our customers accrue in accessing their genetic information outweigh potential risks."[15]

Yet critics charge that genetic testing should not be conducted without medical professionals to help individuals properly understand the results and develop the best treatment or surveillance program. In addition, research shows that some at-home genetic tests are not even accurate. The US Government Accountability Office (GAO) investigated direct-to-consumer genetic tests in 2009. It purchased ten tests from each of four different genetic testing companies and concluded that the results were inaccurate and misleading. In fact, according to Gregory Kutz of the GAO, "Four of our five donors received test results that conflicted with their factual medical conditions and family histories."[16]

Discrimination

Many people are afraid that when the results of genetic tests become available to other people such as health insurance companies and employers, they may be used to discriminate against individuals. For example, a health insurance company may not want to insure an individual if genetic testing reveals that he or she has a chance of developing a genetic disease, because this may mean increased health care costs. The National Human Genome Research Institute warns,

> More and more tests are being developed to find DNA differences that affect our health. Called genetic tests, these tests will become a routine part of health care in the future. Health care providers will use information about each person's DNA to develop more individualized ways of detecting, treating and preventing disease. But unless this DNA information is protected, it could be used to discriminate against people.[17]

As a result of such fears, many people are reluctant to undergo genetic testing, sometimes even if it is recommended by a medical professional. In some cases individuals pay with cash or even use false names in order to protect their privacy. The 2008 Genetic Information Nondiscrimination Act prohibits health insurance companies or employers from discriminating against people on the basis of DNA information. However many people point out that it does not cover discrimination in all situations. For example, the act does not protect people from discrimination in obtaining life insurance, disability insurance, or long-term care insurance.

Gene Therapy

Gene therapy is an experimental technique in which researchers replace or repair abnormal genes in order to treat or prevent disease. While potentially useful, this technique is still under development. The National Library of Medicine explains, "Although gene therapy is a promising treatment option for a number of diseases . . . the technique remains risky and is still under study to make sure that it will be safe and effective. Gene therapy is currently only being tested for the treatment of diseases that have no other cures."[18]

> **Many people believe that genetic testing and manipulation will eventually lead to genetic enhancement.**

Current gene therapy involves altering genes in a person's somatic (body) cells, which means that changes cannot be passed on to his or her offspring. But gene therapy also has the potential to alter genes in germ-line cells (egg and sperm), which would make changes heritable. This possibility is extremely controversial. Proponents maintain that individuals should have the choice to improve their genes if they choose to. However, critics fear that making irreversible changes to genes could cause problems for later generations, is overstepping the bounds of the power humans should have, and is unethical because it takes away the freedom of choice of the next generation. Warn Thomas A. Shannon and Nicholas J. Kockler, "What a particular culture sees as desirable may not be beneficial for the individual recipient, for society, or human beings as a group."[19]

Genetic Enhancement

Many people believe that genetic testing and manipulation will eventually lead to genetic enhancement; for example, choosing a child's hair color or height or manipulating genetics to make a person smarter or more athletic. While some people welcome such possibilities, many believe that these types of enhancement would be unethical. Critics argue that enhancement would objectify children and cause inequality between those who can afford the technology and those who cannot. Richard

Hayes, executive director of the Center for Genetics and Society, asks, "Once we begin genetically modifying our children, where do we stop? If it's acceptable to modify one gene, why not two, or 20 or 200? At what point do children become artifacts designed to someone's specifications rather than members of a family to be nurtured?"[20] In its Code of Medical Ethics, the American Medical Association is opposed to genetic enhancement. It says, "Because of the potential for abuse, genetic manipulation to affect non-disease traits may never be acceptable and perhaps should never be pursued."[21]

As researchers increase the possibilities of genetic testing and manipulation, society expresses mixed opinions. Some people welcome the opportunity to use technology to change their lives and the lives of their children. Others fear that such power is unethical.

Primary Source Quotes*

Can Genetic Testing and Manipulation Be Done Ethically?

66 Genomic science is racing toward a future in which foreseeable improvements include reduced susceptibility to a host of diseases, increased life span, better cognitive functioning and maybe even cosmetic enhancements such as whiter, straighter teeth. . . . I believe that we can and will incorporate gene technology into the ongoing human adventure. 99

—Ronald M. Green, "Building Baby from the Genes Up," *Washington Post*, April 13, 2008. www.washingtonpost.com.

Green is a professor of ethics at Dartmouth College. His most recent book is *Babies by Design: The Ethics of Genetic Choice.*

66 New human genetic technologies . . . have the potential for real harm. If misapplied, they would exacerbate existing inequalities and reinforce existing modes of discrimination. If more widely abused, they could undermine the foundations of civil and human rights. 99

—Richard Hayes, "Genetically Modified Humans? No Thanks," *Washington Post*, April 15, 2008. www.washingtonpost.com.

Hayes is executive director of the Center for Genetics and Society.

* Editor's Note: While the definition of a primary source can be narrowly or broadly defined, for the purposes of Compact Research, a primary source consists of: 1) results of original research presented by an organization or researcher; 2) eyewitness accounts of events, personal experience, or work experience; 3) first-person editorials offering pundits' opinions; 4) government officials presenting political plans and/or policies; 5) representatives of organizations presenting testimony or policy.

❝To investigate DTC [direct-to-consumer] genetic products currently on the market, we purchased tests, for $299 to $999, from a nonrepresentative selection of four of the dozens of genetic testing companies selling kits to consumers on the Internet. . . . The test results we received are misleading and of little or no practical use to consumers.❞

—Gregory Kutz, "Direct-to-Consumer Genetic Tests: Misleading Test Results Are Further Complicated by Deceptive Marketing and Other Questionable Practices," testimony before the Subcommittee on Oversight and Investigations, Committee on Energy and Commerce, House of Representatives, June 22, 2010. www.gao.gov.

Kutz is managing director of Forensic Audits and Special Investigations of the US Government Accountability Office.

❝Customers empowered with this information [from direct-to-consumer genetic testing] have made lifestyle changes aimed at reducing their risks of developing disease and have provided information to their doctors to aid in diagnosis and treatment. These actions have improved and even saved lives.❞

—Ashley C. Gould, "Direct-To-Consumer Genetic Testing and Consequences to the Public Health," congressional testimony before the Committee on Energy and Commerce, Subcommittee on Oversight and Investigations, US House of Representatives, July 22, 2010. http://republicans.energycommerce.house.gov.

Gould is general counsel for personal genetics company 23andMe.

❝PGD [preimplantation genetic diagnosis] is genetic testing with the intent of discarding the human beings that 'fail' the test. This fact alone makes PGD immoral.❞

—Rebecca Taylor, "Ethics of Genetic Testing: Part 2," *Mary Meets Dolly*, January 6, 2009. www.marymeetsdolly.com.

Taylor is a clinical laboratory specialist in molecular biology and creator of the website *Mary Meets Dolly*, which comments on genetics and genetic engineering from a Catholic perspective.

> **❝I don't see any problem with parents choosing an embryo that doesn't have cystic fibrosis or putting a gene into an embryo that protects that child from getting AIDS or heart disease or diabetes or obesity. What I do see, though is the real ethical dilemma that's going to confront us in the future is that this technology is very expensive. People . . . without money are not going to be able to afford it.❞**

—Lee Silver, Q&A interview, "Prenatal Testing: Do You Really Want to Know Your Baby's Future?" *DNA Files*, April 30, 2008. www.dnafiles.org.

Silver is a professor of genetics at Princeton University.

> **❝By eliminating less perfect humans [through genetic screening], deformity and disability become more pronounced and less acceptable. Those who escape the net of screening are often viewed as mistakes or burdens.❞**

—Michael Gerson, "Trig's Breakthrough," *Washington Post*, September 10, 2008. www.washingtonpost.com.

Gerson writes about politics and policy for the *Washington Post*.

> **❝Pre-natal genetic testing, while many of us are told it's a way to help 'prepare' families in cases of adverse diagnosis and help vanish suffering, is a tool, sometimes even propagated by the same types of people who condone eugenics, to eliminate those with disabilities in order to make a more perfect society.❞**

—Kristan Hawkins, "Mom of Disabled Child: Pre-Natal Genetic Testing Can Lead to More Abortions," *LifeNews.com*, February 23, 2010. www.lifenews.com.

Hawkins has a son with cystic fibrosis. She also runs a website dedicated to raising awareness of children with special needs.

Can Genetic Testing and Manipulation Be Done Ethically?

- In a 2009 survey of 1,504 adults living in the United States, the Pew Research Center for the People & the Press found that **53 percent** of respondents believe genetic testing is a change for the better and **13 percent** believe it is a change for the worse.

- The National Down Syndrome Society reports that about **6,000 babies** with Down syndrome are born each year.

- If both parents carry the recessive gene for a genetic disorder, there is a **1 in 4** chance their child will inherit the disorder. If one parent is affected by a disorder caused by a single dominant gene, there is a **1 in 2** chance that a child will inherit the disorder.

- According to the California Pacific Medical Center, preimplantation genetic diagnosis testing is **96 to 98 percent** accurate.

- According to the National Institutes of Health, even with the best care children with **Tay-Sachs disease** usually die by age four.

- In a 2010 survey of 1,000 people age 18 and older, the AARP found that more than **two-thirds** of respondents say they would not consider genetic testing to determine whether they are at increased risk for developing specific inherited diseases.

Growth in Genetic Testing

As genetic testing becomes more prevalent, bioethicists face increasing ethical dilemmas. This chart from GeneTests, a website of the National Center for Biotechnology Information, shows information from its Laboratory Directory. The directory is a listing of US and international laboratories that offer various types of genetic testing. The chart reveals that between 1993 and 2009 there was an increase in both the number of laboratories offering genetic testing and the number of diseases for which testing is available.

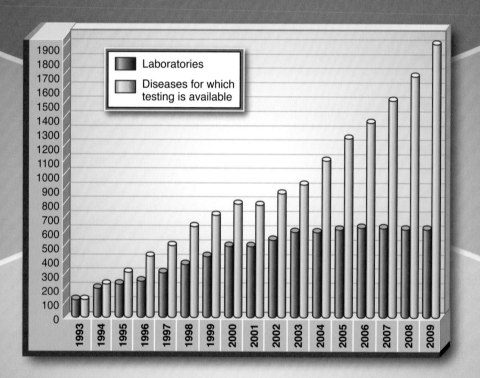

Source: GeneTests,"Laboratory Directory Growth Chart," 2009. www.genetests.org.

- The Federal Trade Commission reports that the prices of at-home genetic tests range from **$295 to $1,200**.

- According to the National Institutes of Health, genetic testing is available for over **2,000 conditions**.

Genetic Screening of Newborns Is Widespread

Genetic screening of newborns has raised an increasing number of ethical concerns as it becomes more widespread and more comprehensive. This map shows the use of genetic screening of newborns in the United States. It reveals that the majority of states screen newborns for more than 40 different harmful disorders, including genetic ones. Arizona and Texas screen for 29 disorders, the least of all the states. By detecting disorders early, doctors have a better chance of treating children.

50+   40–49   39 and under

Source: Lee, "Newborn Screening Saves Lives, *5 Minutes for Special Needs*, March 22, 2011.
www.5minutesforspecialneeds.com.

- The Hastings Center reports that approximately **85 percent** of women terminate their pregnancies following a positive test result for Down syndrome.

Increased Risk Associated with Gene Mutations

Genetic testing can help a person make a more accurate prediction about his or her risk of developing a number of different diseases or disorders. This chart shows how much gene mutations increase the risk for developing various genetic disorders. It lists the risk for someone in the general population for developing breast cancer, ovarian cancer, colon cancer, and Alzheimer's disease, and compares this risk with that of someone with known gene mutations for that disorder. While a gene mutation does not guarantee that people will develop a certain disorder, it does mean that they have a significantly higher chance of doing so.

Disorder	Lifetime Risk for Someone in the General Population	Lifetime Risk for Someone with Known Mutations
Breast cancer	About 12% of women	Between 40% and 80%, depending on the mutation
Ovarian cancer	About 1%	Between 20% and 40%, depending on the mutation
Colon cancer	About 6%	Between 60% and 80%, depending on the mutation
Alzheimer's disease, late-onset form	About 5% by age 70, about 30% by age 85	About 10–25% by age 70, about 50–75% by age 85

Source: Doris Teichler Zallen, *To Test or Not to Test: A Guide to Genetic Screening and Risk.* Piscataway, NJ: Rutgers University Press, 2008.

- NetWellness, a website of the University of Cincinnati, reports that approximately **10 percent** of adults and **30 percent** of children in hospitals are there due to genetically related problems.

At-Home Genetic Tests Yield Contradictory Results

Some people argue that at-home genetic testing is unethical because it produces unreliable results. These charts reveal the results for four donors who participated in an investigation of at-home genetic tests. A sample of each donor's DNA was sent to four different at-home genetic testing companies and, as these results show, the various companies provided contradictory analyses of identical DNA samples.

Gender	Age	Condition	Company 1	Company 2	Company 3	Company 4
Female	37	Leukemia	Above average	Below average	Average	Not tested
		Breast cancer	Average	Above average	Average	Above average
Female	41	Type 1 diabetes	Above average	Above average	Below average	Not tested
		Restless leg syndrome	Below average	Above average	Not tested	Average
Male	48	Prostate cancer	Average	Average	Below average	Above average
		Hypertension	Average	Below average	Above average	Not tested
Male	61	Celiac disease	Above average	Average	Not tested	Above average
		Multiple sclerosis	Below average	Average	Average	Below average

Source: Gregory Kutz, "Direct-to-Consumer Genetic Tests: Misleading Test Results Are Further Complicated by Deceptive Marketing and Other Questionable Practices," testimony before the Subcommittee on Oversight and Investigations, Committee on Energy and Commerce, House of Representatives, June 22, 2010. www.gao.gov.

- The American Society for Reproductive Medicine reports that approximately **7 percent** of stillbirths and deaths within the first 28 days of life are due to chromosomal abnormalities.

- According to the American College of Obstetrics and Gynecologists, approximately 1 in 25 Caucasians is a carrier of **cystic fibrosis.**

Is the Use of Human Embryos in Stem Cell Research Ethical?

> **Stem cell research requiring the destruction of human embryos is objectionable on legal, ethical, and scientific grounds.**
>
> —Center for Bioethics & Human Dignity, a bioethics organization.

> **Human embryonic stem-cell research is not only ethical, it is an essential field to pursue.**
>
> —Dan S. Kaufman, associate director of the University of Minnesota Stem Cell Institute.

In 1995 movie star Christopher Reeve, well known for his role as fictional superhero Superman, suddenly became a quadriplegic after suffering a spinal cord injury in a horse riding accident. Even though his accident left him in a wheelchair, Reeve believed that one day he might walk again. The reason for his hope was embryonic stem cell research, which many scientists believe has the potential to cure a wide range of injuries and illnesses. In 2000 Reeve stated, "These cells have the potential to cure disease and conditions ranging from Parkinson's and MS to diabetes, heart disease, to Alzheimer's, Lou Gehrig's, even spinal cord injuries like my own. . . . They could help save thousands of lives."[22] Reeve died of a heart attack in 2004, with such cures still merely a hope, but many other people continue to strongly advocate embryonic stem cell research. However, this research also provokes controversy because it involves the destruction of human embryos, and the debate continues over whether it is ethical.

Embryos and Human Life

One of the biggest controversies over embryonic stem cell research is whether it is ethical to destroy a human embryo. Embryonic stem cells are usually taken from an early embryo called a blastocyst that is about four or five days old and is comprised of about 150 cells. Taking the cells for research means the destruction of the embryo. Some people argue that at this early stage of development the embryo is not a human life but merely a collection of undifferentiated cells with the potential to become a life. They believe that it does not deserve the same rights as a human being and that using cells from this early embryo for research is ethical.

> " One of the biggest controversies over embryonic stem cell research is whether it is ethical to destroy a human embryo. "

Others insist that no matter how small it is, an embryo is a human being and it is unethical to destroy it. Explains the US Conference of Catholic Bishops, "The human embryo, from conception onward, is as much a living member of the human species as any of us. As a matter of biological fact, this new living organism has the full complement of human genes and is actively expressing those genes to live and develop in a way that is unique to human beings."[23]

Embryos Discarded from Fertility Clinics

One way to obtain embryonic stem cells for research is to use those not needed by fertility clinics. During fertility treatments, clinics create more embryos than needed and later discard those left over. The controversy is about whether using these embryos for research is ethical. Some people believe it is since they would otherwise be destroyed. Said Reeve, "I do not understand why . . . there is a huge issue about it, now that discarded embryos will be used for research instead of just being thrown into the garbage."[24]

The American Society for Reproductive Medicine is one of many organizations that believes it is ethically acceptable to use excess embryos for research if that research is likely to provide significant new knowledge, is conducted in a way that gives the embryo respect, and the donor gives his or her informed consent. Others maintain that no matter what the potential benefits, using human embryos for research is unethical. The US Conference of Catholic Bishops maintains, "Some claim that scientists who kill embryos for their stem cells are not actually depriving anyone of life, because they are using 'spare' or unwanted embryos who will die anyway. This argument is simply invalid. Ultimately each of us will die, but that gives no one a right to kill us."[25]

Existing Stem Cell Lines

Some stem cell research is conducted using embryonic stem cells from existing lines, but there is disagreement over whether this is a good source of cells. A line is created when researchers take stem cells from an embryo, then keep the cells replicating in a laboratory for a long period of time. Between 2001 and 2009 US policy stated that federal funding for embryonic stem cell research was allowed only for existing lines. A White House press release from 2001 explains the reason for this policy, stating that using existing lines allowed scientists to pursue potentially lifesaving research without destroying embryos because "the embryos from which the existing stem cell lines were created have already been destroyed and no longer have the possibility of further development as human beings."[26] Yet some people were critical of this policy because they believe these lines do not have enough genetic diversity. Explains the University of Minnesota Stem Cell Institute, "Existing stem cell lines represent only a tiny fraction of the human gene pool; they do not represent the diversity of the human population or the diversity of human illness."[27] Others question the safety of these lines for human research, since most of them were grown in culture with the help of mouse stem cells, and this raises the possibility that they could pass animal viruses on to people.

> " Researchers believe that embryonic stem cell research has the potential to illuminate understanding of the way the human body works. "

Research Potential

Because all cells in the body originate from stem cells, researchers believe that embryonic stem cell research has the potential to illuminate understanding of the way the human body works. Such research might also lead to the development of treatments for cells that become unhealthy. Explains the Harvard Stem Cell Institute,

> Stem cells offer the possibility of a renewable source of replacement cells to treat a wide variety of diseases and disabilities, including diabetes, neurological disease, cardiovascular disease, blood disease and many other conditions. . . . Defective stem cells also appear to underlie many forms of cancer, and by understanding their properties it should be possible to develop new types of anti-cancer therapy.[28]

Critics argue that the potential benefits of embryonic stem cell research have been exaggerated and that many obstacles have to be overcome before the hoped-for cures become a reality. The Center for Bioethics & Human Dignity says, "Though embryonic stem cells have been purported as holding great medical promise, reports of actual clinical success have been few. Instead, scientists conducting research on embryonic stem cells have encountered significant obstacles—including tumor formation . . . and an inability to stimulate the cells to form the desired type of tissue."[29]

Public Funding for Stem Cell Research

Whether public funding should be used for embryonic stem cell research is a controversial issue in the United States and has caused ongoing legal debate. The 1996 Dickey-Wicker Amendment prohibits federal dollars from being used to support any studies in which human embryos are harmed, though a later ruling states that embryonic stem cells are not the same thing as embryos. So researchers have used private funds to create lines—the part of the research in which embryos are destroyed—then used federal funds to study those existing lines.

The American Association for the Advancement of Science argues that federal funding is an important part of exploring the great potential of embryonic stem cell research. It insists, "Only through federal support of diverse avenues of stem cell research, including especially embryonic stem cell research . . . we may better understand the potential value and limitations of each approach."[30] However, critics argue against such funding because they believe this research is unethical.

Adult Stem Cells

Some people argue that embryonic stem cell research is actually unnecessary because research with adult stem cells has just as much potential. Adult stem cells are undifferentiated cells found in various parts of the body such as the bone marrow or the heart. If that part of the body is damaged through injury or disease, these stems cells can differentiate into the various types of cells needed as a replacement. Francis S. Collins, director of the National Institutes of Health, explains that adult stem cells are an important source of research: "NIH is strongly committed to research using adult stem cells. . . . NIH has invested many hundreds of millions of dollars over the years in adult stem cell research. Indeed, annually we are spending almost three times as much on adult stem cell research as on human embryonic stem cell research."[31]

> **Most researchers believe that while adult stem cell research has great potential, it is not a replacement for embryonic stem cell research.**

However, most researchers believe that while adult stem cell research has great potential, it is not a replacement for embryonic stem cell research. Adult stem cells can only differentiate into a limited number of different types of cells, depending on where they are found in the body. For example, adult stem cells from the heart can only differentiate into different types of heart cells. Another problem is that they are more difficult to obtain for research because they are relatively rare in adult tissues and do not seem to have the same capacity to multiply in a laboratory culture as embryonic stem cells do.

Induced Pluripotent Stem Cells

Embryonic stems cells are valuable to researchers because they are pluripotent, meaning that they are able to differentiate into all cell types. However, in 2006 researchers successfully created pluripotent cells in the laboratory by reprogramming ordinary, nonpluripotent skin cells. Called induced pluripotent stem (iPS) cells, these are adult cells that are altered to have the properties of embryonic stem cells. There is disagreement over whether they are a good substitute for embryonic stem cells.

Many researchers maintain that while IPS cells are extremely promising, how safe they are and whether they are actually the same as embryonic stem cells is still unclear. Thus they argue that embryonic stem cell research is still needed for comparison. Says the Harvard Stem Cell Institute, "Embryonic stem cells remain the gold standard. If iPS technology (often referred to as 'reprogramming') is to eventually replace embryonic stem cells in research, it will be because the results were compared and refined against stem cells from a true embryonic source."[32]

> **There is disagreement over whether [induced pluripotent stem cells] are a good substitute for embryonic stem cells.**

Yet some critics argue that the insistence on continuing to use embryonic stem cells is more about politics and personal preference than science, with researchers reluctant to give up something they have spent so much time and money researching. Stem cell research expert Joseph Panno says, "The reluctance of the science community to let go of human ES cell research sounds like an empire builder's lament: So much time and energy has been put into it, so much money has been spent on it, so many careers have depended on it—we cannot let it go."[33]

In fiscal year 2010, approximately $137 million in federal funds was appropriated by the National Institutes of Health for embryonic stem cell research. As this number reveals, this is a significant field of research. Yet despite such investment, the debate about the ethics of embryonic stem cell research continues.

Primary Source Quotes*

Is the Use of Human Embryos in Stem Cell Research Ethical?

66 The majority of Americans . . . have come to a consensus that we should pursue this [embryonic stem cell] research. That the potential it offers is great, and with proper guidelines and strict oversight, the perils can be avoided. 99

—Barack Obama, "Signing of Stem Cell Executive Order and Scientific Integrity Presidential Memorandum," Washington DC, March 9, 2009.

Obama is the forty-fourth president of the United States.

66 We should not create human life, create an embryo and then destroy it for research, if there are other options out there. . . . And thankfully, again, not only are there other options, but we're getting closer and closer to finding a tremendous amount more of options. 99

—Sarah Palin, interview by Charlie Gibson, *ABC News*, September 11, 2008. http://abcnews.go.com.

Palin is a politician and former governor of Alaska.

Bracketed quotes indicate conflicting positions.

* Editor's Note: While the definition of a primary source can be narrowly or broadly defined, for the purposes of Compact Research, a primary source consists of: 1) results of original research presented by an organization or researcher; 2) eyewitness accounts of events, personal experience, or work experience; 3) first-person editorials offering pundits' opinions; 4) government officials presenting political plans and/or policies; 5) representatives of organizations presenting testimony or policy.

Primary Source Quotes

66 **Whether scientists want to admit it or not, iPS [induced pluripotent stem cells], with their infinite potential, have already made . . . human ES cell research obsolete.** 99

—Joseph Panno, *Stem Cell Research*. New York: Facts On File, 2010, p. 87.

Panno is the author of numerous books about biotechnology, including *Stem Cell Research: Medical Applications and Ethical Controversies.*

66 **Some opposed to hESC research have argued that we don't need hES cells anymore, now that iPS cells have been developed. But . . . to devise new therapies, research must continue with all types of stem cells. If we allow research on hES cells to wither, who knows how many other breakthroughs, like adult cell reprogramming, will go undiscovered.** 99

—Coalition for the Advancement of Medical Research, "A Catalyst for Cures: Embryonic Stem Cell Research," January 12, 2009. www.camradvocacy.org.

The Coalition for the Advancement of Medical Research is an organization that focuses on developing better treatments and cures for people with life-threatening illnesses and disorders.

66 **Stem cells from adult tissues . . . can be obtained without harm to the donor and without any ethical problem, and these have already demonstrated great medical promise.** 99

—US Conference of Catholic Bishops, "On Embryonic Stem Cell Research," June 2008. www.usccb.org.

The US Conference of Catholic Bishops is an organization that aims to coordinate and promote Catholic activities in the United States.

66 **Adult stem cells are less than ideal for many types of research and therapy because they do not divide indefinitely in culture, and they produce only a limited number of cells and cell types.** 99

—Francis S. Collins, congressional testimony before the Senate Subcommittee on Labor—HHS—Education Appropriations," September 16, 2010. www.nih.gov.

Collins is director of the National Institutes of Health, the government agency dedicated to protecting the health of Americans.

❝I was a healthy 12-year-old kid who was very active and had big dreams. Everything changed on February 5, 1999. . . . In a manner of 20 minutes my body became paralyzed and my life drastically changed. . . . [Embryonic stem cell] research is real, promising and hopeful to me and others.❞

—Cody Unser, congressional testimony, "The Promise of Embryonic Stem Cells: Senator Tom Harkin Hearing," September 16, 2010.

Unser is a public health graduate student at George Washington University. She suffers from transverse myelitis and is confined to a wheelchair.

❝The long-desired end, that human embryonic stem cell research would find cures for a multitude of diseases, has not become a reality. . . . Embryonic stem-cell research has produced zero cures or treatments for humans.❞

—William Saunders, "Another Unethical and Unsound Idea, Brought to You by the Federal Government," *Catholic Thing*, March 16, 2010. www.thecatholicthing.org.

Saunders is senior vice president of legal affairs at pro-life organization Americans United for Life.

❝Requiring the destruction of embryos—the tiniest human beings—embryonic stem cell research violates the medical ethic, 'Do No Harm.'❞

—Focus on the Family, "Our Position (Stem Cells)," 2009. www.focusonthefamily.com.

Focus on the Family is a global Christian ministry dedicated to helping families thrive.

❝Human embryos are not full human persons. . . . Human embryos have intermediate moral status requiring special respect, that need not be incompatible with using and destroying them for medical research that has reasonable promise to understand, treat, or prevent serious human disease and suffering.❞

—Dan W. Brock, "Creating Embryos for Use in Stem Cell Research," *Journal of Law, Medicine & Ethics*, Summer 2010. www.aslme.org.

Brock is director of the Division of Medical Ethics at the Harvard Medical School and the director of the Harvard University Program in Ethics and Health.

Facts and Illustrations

Is the Use of Human Embryos in Stem Cell Research Ethical?

- In a 2010 survey of 1,028 people living in the United States, Gallup found that **59 percent** of respondents believe medical research using stem cells obtained from human embryos is morally acceptable while **32 percent** believe it is morally wrong.

- The National Institutes of Health reports that in 2010 it provided **$40 million** in support of human embryonic stem cell research.

- In the United States, according to a 2011 report by the James A. Baker III Institute for Public Policy, 18 states have legislation in effect that **prohibits embryonic stem cell research**.

- Between 2001 and 2009 an executive order issued by President George W. Bush allowed federal funding for human embryonic stem cell research using only **21 existing lines**.

- According to *Newsweek*, in 2010 the Harvard Stem Cell Institute received **450 donated embryos** for research purposes.

- The National Institutes of Health reports that adult stem cells from **bone marrow** have been used in transplants for approximately 40 years.

State Stem Cell Policies Vary

This map classifies varying state policies on stem cell research as restrictive, moderate, permissive, or undecided. The majority of states are either moderate or undecided. Permissive states include Washington, California, New York, and Wisconsin. Restrictive states include Arizona, North and South Dakota, Oklahoma, and Pennsylvania. In total, 18 states prohibit embryonic stem cell research.

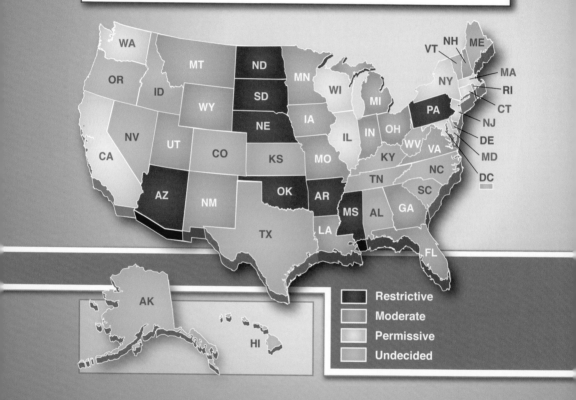

Restrictive
Moderate
Permissive
Undecided

Source: James A. Baker Institute for Public Policy, "Stem Cells and Biomedical Research Found in Texas," January 2011. www.bakerinstitute.org.

- In a 2008 study from Duke University Medical Center, 1,000 couples who had frozen embryos in storage at fertility clinics were surveyed and **12 percent** said they preferred to discard the embryos rather than donate them for research.

Majority of Americans Support Embryonic Stem Cell Research

This graph compares the results of Gallup polls between 2003 and 2010 that investigate the opinion of the American public on embryonic stem cell research. It shows that while support has fluctuated, overall the majority of Americans do support embryonic stem cell research.

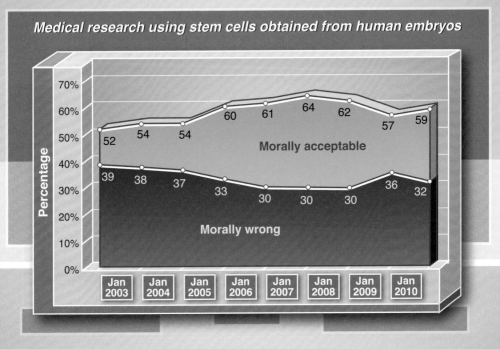

Medical research using stem cells obtained from human embryos

Source: Gallup, "Americans and Embryonic Stem Cell Research," August 24, 2010. http://pollingmatters.gallup.com.

- In a 2009 survey of 2,001 Americans, the Pew Research Center found that **58 percent** of people favor federal funding for embryonic stem cell research and **35 percent** are opposed.

- The James A. Baker III Institute for Public Policy estimates that the number of patients treated with stem cell therapies will increase from **20,000** in 2007 to **9.4 million** in 2020.

Non-Embryonic Stem Cell Research Receives More Federal Funds

This chart shows NIH funding for various types of stem cell research between 2007 and 2010, with estimates for 2011 and 2012. It reveals that non-embryonic stem cell research receives greater funding than embryonic stem cell research, which is more controversial and more strictly regulated. While funding for all types of research increased between 2007 and 2010, the NIH does not project large increases for 2011 and 2012.

Research Area	Dollars in Millions					
	FY 2007	FY 2008	FY 2009	FY 2010	FY 2011 Estimated	FY 2012 Estimated
Embryonic Stem Cell Research	$74	$88	$120	$126	$125	$128
Non-Embryonic Stem Cell Research	$226	$297	$339	$341	$341	$347

Source: National Institutes of Health, "Estimates for Funding for Various Research, Condition, and Disease Categories," February 14, 2011.

- In 2004 California voters passed Proposition 71, which provides **$3 billion** for embryonic stem cell research over ten years.

- According to the National Institutes of Health, in 2011 three existing **clinical trials** were using cells derived from human embryonic stem cells.

Support for Federally Funded Embryonic Stem Cell Research Has Increased

These two graphs compare US public opinion in 2005 and 2009 on expanded federal funding for embryonic stem cell research. The number of people strongly in favor of expanded funding stayed about the same, while those somewhat in favor increased, meaning an overall increase of those in favor of expanded funding.

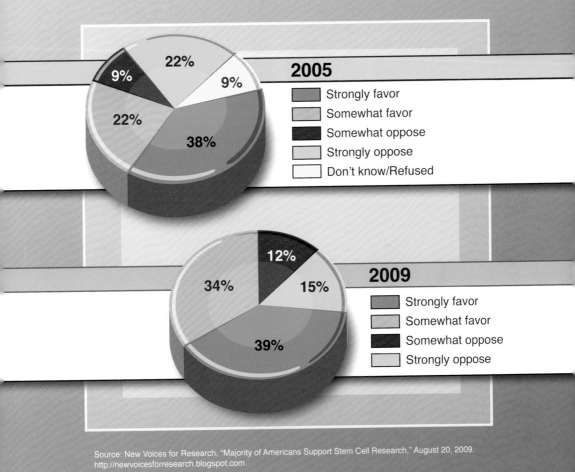

2005

- Strongly favor
- Somewhat favor
- Somewhat oppose
- Strongly oppose
- Don't know/Refused

22% 9% 9% 22% 38%

2009

- Strongly favor
- Somewhat favor
- Somewhat oppose
- Strongly oppose

12% 15% 34% 39%

Source: New Voices for Research, "Majority of Americans Support Stem Cell Research," August 20, 2009. http://newvoicesforresearch.blogspot.com.

- According to *Tell Me About Stem Cells*, a website created by Harvard and the Massachusetts Institute of Technology, stem cell research has the potential to help over **100 million Americans**.

Is Assisted Reproductive Technology Ethical?

66 Assisted reproductive technologies (ART) have enabled millions of people in the world to have biological children who otherwise would not have been able to do so. 99

—Emily Galpern, Center for Genetics and Society.

66 We have the power to control human reproduction as never before. The question is: Should we? 99

—Lewis Vaughn, ethicist.

In January 2008 Nadya Suleman, a 33-year-old unemployed single mother of six from Southern California, gave birth to octuplets after in vitro fertilization. While medical technology makes such a birth possible, whether it is ethical is open to debate. Many people argue that it was irresponsible for Suleman's doctor to facilitate this birth, considering that Suleman already had six children and a limited income with which to care for them. In addition, a pregnancy with octuplets risks the health of both the mother and babies and incurs hundreds of thousands of dollars in medical bills. Suleman's case provoked widespread debate on the ethics of assisted reproductive technology which, though widespread in the United States and elsewhere, remains controversial.

Who Should Be Allowed to Have a Baby?

Before the development of reproductive technologies such as in vitro fertilization and surrogacy, if a woman was unable to become pregnant and give birth to a child, the only other way to have a child was by adoption. However, now many people who cannot have a baby naturally can be biological parents with the help of laboratory manipulation. In addition to heterosexual couples who are unable to conceive, other groups of people such as same-sex couples, who would not otherwise be able to have a child, are using this technology. As researcher Timothy F. Murphy explains, "More and more people who never would have had children in the past are now doing so: postmenopausal women who gestate children, infertile heterosexual couples relying on donor gametes and donor embryos, same-sex couples doing the same, single men and women of all sexual orientations turning to surrogate mothers."[34] However, while technology now allows all these people to have children, questions remain about whether it is ethical. The American Society for Reproductive Medicine maintains that fertility doctors should not discriminate on the basis of sexual orientation or marital status. It says, "We believe that the ethical duty to treat persons with equal respect requires that fertility programs treat single persons and gay and lesbian couples equally to heterosexual couples in determining which services to provide."[35]

Yet some people do object to certain groups such as single parents or homosexual couples using fertility treatment to have children. In some cases fertility clinics have denied treatment because of the doctors' beliefs. For example, in 2000 Guadalupe Benitez, a lesbian, sued a California fertility clinic that refused to perform artificial insemination for her. She argued that the doctors were discriminating against her on the basis of her sexual orientation. The doctors argued that they had a religious objection to providing treatment to her. In 2008 the California Supreme Court ruled in favor of Benitez, stating that she had a right to receive medical services without discrimination.

> " Assisted reproductive technology . . . though widespread in the United States and elsewhere, remains controversial. "

Objectification of Children

Critics argue that assisted reproductive technology objectifies children, meaning that it encourages society to view children as manufactured products that can be purchased for a price. Using technology to create life in a laboratory, and sometimes even selecting certain traits during the process, raises serious ethical questions for some. Critics such as philosopher Michael J. Sandel argue that instead of creating children in a laboratory, society should appreciate them as gifts. He explains, "To appreciate children as gifts is to accept them as they come, not as objects of our design, or products of our will, or instruments of our ambition."[36]

> Some people do object to certain groups such as single parents or homosexual couples using fertility treatment to have children.

Others maintain that just because a child is conceived with assisted reproductive technology, there is no reason to believe that his or her parents will value that child any less. James Hughes, executive director of the Institute for Ethics and Emerging Technologies, says that critics should not be so quick to criticize those people who use assisted reproductive technology to create children, because these parents usually have good intentions. He says, "If parents provide food, exercise and education for children to ensure that they are smart and healthy we praise them as responsible. When they try to ensure the same goods for their children with reproductive technology we imply that they have twisted, malign, instrumental values."[37]

Complicated Family Relationships

As assisted reproductive technology increases the possibilities of how a child can be created, it complicates the definitions of parenthood and family. In the past only a man and woman could conceive a child through sexual relations with one another, and a family has traditionally comprised a man, a woman, and their children. However as Lewis Vaughn explains, the definition of parenthood has changed as assisted reproductive technology has expanded the possibilities of who can parent a child. He says, "Through ART, a child can have many parents—genetic (those who contribute egg or sperm), gestational (the woman who carries the baby to term), and social (the people who raise the child). With all these possibilities, the family can take forms that were unthinkable a few decades ago."[38]

Health Risks

Some research shows that assisted reproductive technology is associated with a greater number of health risks than natural conception. Assisted reproductive technology does result in a greater number of twin and multiple births than natural conception, and for this reason, it is associated with increased health risks to both mothers and babies. According to the CDC, multiple-infant births are riskier because they are associated with higher rates of caesarean section, prematurity, low birth weight, and infant disability or death. The National Conference of State Legislatures reports that an increase in multiple births has led to an increase in prematurity. It says that in 2007, 8.2 percent of all newborns were low–birth-weight (less than 5.5 pounds), the highest percentage since the early 1970s. This increased prematurity and the health problems that frequently come with it impact more than just the parents of these children. The organization finds that preterm births cost society at least $26 billion per year, primarily due to increased health care and education costs and lost productivity.

Some studies also indicate that children born through assisted reproduction may have a greater risk of birth defects or other health problems. For example, in 2008 the Centers for Disease Control reported the results of a study of 9,584 babies with birth defects and 4,742 without. The study finds that babies conceived by in vitro fertilization have a slightly greater chance of a number of birth defects including a hole in the heart and cleft lip or palate. In the opinion of Richard M. Schultz, associate dean for the natural sciences at the University of Pennsylvania, "There is a growing consensus in the clinical community that there are risks."[39] Yet Schultz and

> " Critics argue that assisted reproductive technology objectifies children. "

others acknowledge that the extent of these risks is not well understood and advocate more research.

Financial Costs

While assisted reproductive technology is often praised because it allows many people to have a baby when they otherwise could not, it is also widely critiqued because many people do not have access to it for financial reasons. Assisted reproductive technology is expensive, and it is not covered by many insurance plans. This means that a limited number of people can afford it. Explains bioethicist David Lemberg, "It's likely that many couples will need to undergo at least two rounds of IVF, spending a minimum of $30,000 and possibly more than $50,000 in attempts to have a family. As the median household income in the United States was approximately $50,000 in 2008, it's obvious that very few families can afford what reproductive medicine has to offer." Lemberg concludes, "The vast majority of families that could benefit from ART are denied access because the procedures are out of reach financially."[40] Many people believe such unequal access is unethical.

Surrogacy

Gestational surrogacy occurs when a surrogate gestates a fetus for another person because that person is unable or unwilling to do so. The surrogate enters into an agreement to carry the pregnancy, then give up the baby at birth for adoption by the intended parents. Surrogates are often paid a fee. Surrogacy laws vary throughout the United States, and some states do not even allow it. It is also controversial. Because surrogates usually receive a fee, opponents argue that surrogacy is unethical because it amounts to selling babies. Advocates contend that surrogates have a right to choose to perform this service and to be paid for it.

Many people do express concern over the lack of government regulation of surrogacy. Because it is not very strictly regulated, it is not uncommon for surrogacy cases to end in conflict, for example with a surrogate mother attempting to keep the baby herself after giving birth to it. Arthur Caplan says, "There are more laws in the United States governing the breeding of dogs, cats, fish, exotic animals, and wild game species than exist with respect to the use of surrogates and reproductive technologies to make people."[41] Caplan and others argue that increased regulation is necessary in order to prevent harm to children, parents, and surrogates.

Rather than finding a surrogate in their own country, an increasing number of people from around the world are traveling to India to hire Indian women to be surrogate mothers because the process is cheaper and legally simpler there. At present surrogate mothers in India have no rights to the child after he or she is born, and only the names of the genetic parents appear on the birth certificate. In addition, surrogacy in India costs half, or even a quarter, the price of what it does in the United States. In a 2010 *Time* magazine article, Nayna Patel, medical director of Akanksha Infertility Clinic in Anand, India, discusses surrogacy there. She says that an increasing number of for-eigners are using her clinic, from only 13 for-eign clients in 2006 to 85 in 2009. According to Patel, the cost is approximately $23,000, of which the surrogate receives $7,500.

Critics argue that Indian surrogacy ex-ploits poor Indian women and risks their health. Many Indians do ostracize surro-gates, so surrogates often hide their pregnan-cies by temporarily moving away from home. Some clinics actually force surrogates to leave home and stay in clinic housing where they

> " Many people express con-cern over the lack of government regulation of surrogacy. "

can be monitored, receive proper nourishment, and avoid risks such as secondhand cigarette smoke. Proponents of Indian surrogacy maintain that it allows many women a way out of the poverty they are otherwise unable to escape. For example, surrogate Sofia Vohra explains that before she became a surrogate she earned $25 a month at a job crushing glass. She says, "[Surrogacy] is not exploitation. Crushing glass for 15 hours a day is exploitation."[42]

An Important Issue for Many People

When conception does not happen naturally some people are willing to pay thousands of dollars in order to have a biologically related child through assisted reproduction techniques such as in vitro fertilization or surrogacy. However, while technology continues to make these tech-niques easier and less expensive, it has not reduced the number of ethical questions that accompany them.

Primary Source Quotes*

Is Assisted Reproductive Technology Ethical?

66 The negligent absence of legal regulation and enforcement [of assisted reproductive technology] in the United States leaves too many women, children, and families at risk. 99

—Connie Cho, "Regulating Assisted Reproductive Technology," *Yale Journal of Medicine and Law*, October 20, 2010. www.yalemedlaw.com.

Connie Cho is a sophomore political science major in Silliman College at Yale University.

66 [Sometimes] the public, spurred by sensationalized media coverage and largely unaware of the way medical practice is regulated in the United States, calls out for additional legal enforcements and punishments. . . . It is important to recognize that ART [assisted reproductive technology] is already one of the most highly regulated of all medical practices in the United States. 99

—American Society for Reproductive Medicine, "Oversight of Assisted Reproductive Technology," 2010. www.asrm.org.

The American Society for Reproductive Medicine is a multidisciplinary organization dedicated to the advancement of the art, science, and practice of reproductive medicine.

Bracketed quotes indicate conflicting positions.

* Editor's Note: While the definition of a primary source can be narrowly or broadly defined, for the purposes of Compact Research, a primary source consists of: 1) results of original research presented by an organization or researcher; 2) eyewitness accounts of events, personal experience, or work experience; 3) first-person editorials offering pundits' opinions; 4) government officials presenting political plans and/or policies; 5) representatives of organizations presenting testimony or policy.

" There does seem to be something wrong about deliberately bringing a child into the world without a mother and a father married to each other. IVF [in vitro fertilization] has been central to such innovations as lesbian parenting. "

—Ramesh Ponnuru, "Out of the Freezer," *National Review*, April 6, 2009. www.nationalreview.com.

Ponnuru is a journalist.

" Over the last 29 years I have been instrumental in assisting more than 100 same sex couples have IVF babies and I can truly testify that in my experience they have usually turned out to make exemplary parents. . . . Frankly, in my opinion, same-sex couples who decide to have a family together often give the issue much more sober consideration than is the case for many heterosexual couples. "

—Geoffrey Sher, "IVF in the 21st Century: Is it Just to Discriminate on the Basis of a Woman's Age, Marital Status, Sexual Preference or the Size of Her Pocketbook?" *IVF Authority*, June 1, 2010. www.ivfauthority.com.

Sher is cofounder and executive medical director of the Sher Institutes for Reproductive Medicine. He practices IVF full time in his Las Vegas office.

" Surrogacy is not a business for brokering or money. It is truly a matter of the heart. . . . I do this out of love. "

—Beverly, comment on "Surrogacy: Wombs for Rent?" PBS, September 18, 2009. www.pbs.org.

Beverly is a surrogate mother and also mother to three children of her own.

" Surrogate motherhood is always ethically and morally wrong. . . . In surrogacy, a child is commissioned (often purchased outright) as if he is a sculpture or a book rather than a human being. "

—Robyn Broyles, "The Ethics of Surrogate Mothers," *Leave the Lights On*, December 22, 2008. www.leavethelightson.info.

Broyles is a writer and mother who lives in Texas.

66 Full reproductive freedom requires . . . a publicly financed health care system that includes fertility treatments, contraception, abortion, prenatal diagnosis, and future reproductive therapies as a right of citizenship. 99

—James Hughes, "What Are Reproductive Rights?" *Institute for Ethics and Emerging Technologies*, August 13, 2010. http://ieet.org.

Hughes is executive director of the Institute for Ethics and Emerging Technologies and teaches health policy at Trinity College in Hartford, Connecticut.

66 One serious problem is that treatment can cause you to get pregnant with multiples (twins, triplets or more). Multiples are more likely to be premature (before 37 completed weeks of pregnancy). Premature babies are at risk of breathing, vision and hearing problems. Being pregnant with multiples also can cause problems for the mother. 99

—March of Dimes, "Trying to Get Pregnant," September 2008. www.marchofdimes.com.

The March of Dimes is an organization that aims to help mothers have full-term pregnancies and research the problems that threaten the health of babies.

Is Assisted Reproductive Technology Ethical?

- According to a 2010 report by the American Society for Reproductive Medicine, approximately **one in every 100** babies born in the United States is conceived using assisted reproductive technology.

- The most recent data from the CDC shows that the number of assisted reproductive technology cycles performed in the United States has nearly doubled, from 81,438 cycles in 1998 to **142,435** in 2007. This technology involves combining egg and sperm in the laboratory, then returning the fertilized egg to the uterus.

- The Centers for Disease Control and Prevention estimates that assisted reproductive technology accounts for slightly more than **1 percent** of total US births.

- According to a 2010 report by the European Society of Human Reproduction and Embryology, the average price of in vitro fertilization treatment in Japan is **$4,012** while in the United States it is approximately **$13,775**.

- In 2008 the Centers for Disease Control and Prevention published the results of a study of 9,584 babies born with birth defects and 4,792 without. Among the mothers of babies without birth defects, **1.1 percent** had used in vitro fertilization or related methods, compared with **2.4 percent** of mothers of babies with birth defects.

Use of Assisted Reproductive Technology Is Increasing

This chart shows that the use of assisted reproductive technology in the United States is increasing. Assisted reproductive technology involves combining eggs and sperm in the laboratory, then returning the fertilized egg to the uterus. The most common type of assisted reproductive technology in the United States is in vitro fertilization. Between 1998 and 2007 the number of assisted reproductive technology procedures performed almost doubled, and there was a large increase in the number of infants born using this technology.

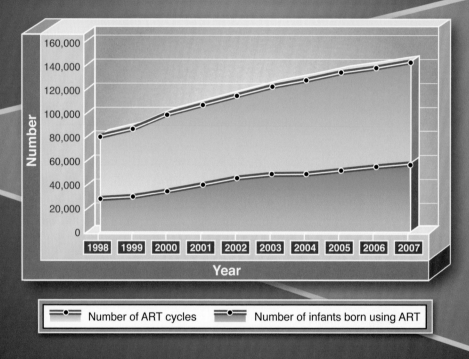

Source: Centers for Disease Control and Prevention, "Assisted Reproductive Technology Success Rates: National Summary and Fertility Clinic Reports," December 2009. www.cdc.gov.

- According to a 2009 report by the American Society for Reproductive Medicine, in 2007 almost **40 percent** of births in the United States were to unmarried women.

Most States Do Not Require Infertility Coverage

The majority of states do not require health insurers to offer plans with fertility coverage. The map shows that only 12 states mandate that all health insurance plans regulated by the state must cover infertility diagnosis and treatment. California and Texas require that every insurer offer at least one plan with fertility coverage.

States Mandating Infertility Insurance Coverage

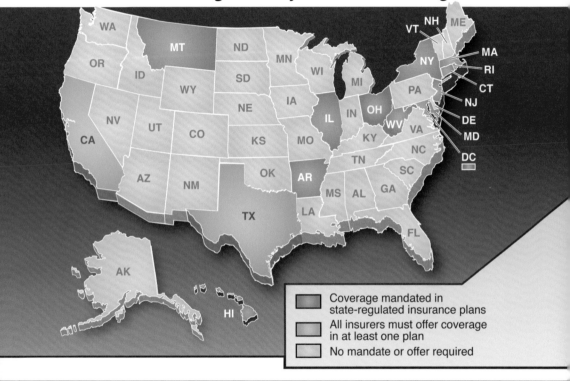

Legend:
- Coverage mandated in state-regulated insurance plans
- All insurers must offer coverage in at least one plan
- No mandate or offer required

Source: Marcia Clemmitt, "Reproductive Ethics," *CQ Researcher*, May 15, 2009. www.cqresearcher.com.

- The American Society for Reproductive Medicine reports that in the United States, infertility affects about 7.3 million women and their partners, or about **12 percent** of the reproductive-aged population.

Many States Have Unclear Surrogacy Laws

This map shows the types of surrogacy laws that each state has. While surrogacy is permitted in many states, a large number of states do not have a clear legal position on surrogacy. Four states prohibit surrogacy, and five states consider surrogacy agreements unenforceable by law.

Permitted—legally permitted, with certain restrictions

Unclear—no laws regarding surrogacy, or ambiguous laws

Unenforceable—surrogacy agreements are deemed unenforceable by law

Prohibited—prohibited by law

Source: California Surrogacy, "Where Is Surrogacy Legal in the US?," 2011. http:/california-surrogacy.com.

- The Medical Tourism Corporation reports that the cost of its surrogacy package, through which a person pays an Indian surrogate to carry a baby for him or her, is about **$22,000 to $35,000**.

- The Hastings Center estimates that in the United States it costs approximately **$50,000** to have a child through surrogacy.

- According to a 2008 BBC report, only **3.3 percent** of in vitro fertilization cycles performed in the United States involve the transfer of only a single embryo; most involve multiple embryos, which frequently leads to pregnancy with multiples.

- In a 2009 report *CQ Researcher* estimates that since 1978 almost **3 million** babies have been born through assisted reproductive technologies worldwide.

- In 2009 the Centers for Disease Control reported that there were **483 assisted reproductive technology clinics** in the United States.

Should Doctors Be Allowed to Help Patients Die?

> **Alongside access to high quality care and treatment, dying adults who can make the decision of their own free will, should have the choice of an assisted death, within strict legal safeguards.**
>
> —Dignity in Dying, UK organization that supports physician-assisted suicide.

> **People who are dying and disabled need love, inclusion and medical care that values their lives, not hastens their deaths.**
>
> —Wesley J. Smith, attorney and journalist.

In 1998 Michigan doctor Jack Kevorkian was convicted of murder after injecting lethal drugs into 52-year-old Thomas Youk, a man suffering from Lou Gehrig's disease. As in most US states, assisted suicide is illegal in Michigan, and Kevorkian spent eight years in prison as a result of his conviction. Yet throughout his sentence and after his release, Kevorkian continued to advocate legalizing assisted suicide. Until his death in 2011, he insisted people should have the right to choose to die, and claimed he has assisted at least 130 people in ending their lives. He said, "It's got to be legalized."[43] Kevorkian was a central figure in the impassioned debate over whether doctors should be allowed to help patients die.

Physician-Assisted Suicide

In physician-assisted suicide a person takes his or her own life with the assistance of a physician. In most cases the physician prescribes a lethal dose of drugs or explains a method of suicide, and the patient is the one to commit the act that causes death. Usually, the person requesting suicide has a fatal illness and is suffering from a poor quality of life.

There are impassioned arguments both for and against physician-assisted suicide. Supporters argue that a person suffering from an incurable illness should have the choice to end that pain. One advocate of physician-assisted suicide on the Death with Dignity National Center website explains, "My younger sister suffocated to death from lung cancer. . . . Her death was anything but dignified. The suffering and humiliation as her organs shut down were inhumane. My dog had a better death only a few months earlier. I don't know if she would have chosen to use the act, but I wish she'd had the choice."[44] However, opponents insist that it is never ethical for a doctor to aid in ending a life, and that legalizing physician-assisted suicide will only lead to harm.

> **There are impassioned arguments both for and against physician-assisted suicide.**

Autonomy

When considering whether doctors should be allowed to help patients end their lives, many people raise the issue of autonomy, the right to control one's own body. Others disagree over whether the right to autonomy should extend to choosing death. Some people argue that each person tolerates pain and psychological distress in different ways and makes different judgments about whether his or her life is worth living. Therefore, each person should have the right to decide whether to end his or her own life. Yet critics insist that autonomy does not include the right to have a medical professional assist in one's death. Neurosurgeon Michael Egnor argues that autonomy means the right to accept or refuse medical treatments, but, he maintains, physician-assisted suicide is not a medical treatment. He says, "The intentional taking of human life—one's own or that of another—is never medical treatment, and is never ethical."[45]

The Slippery Slope

One argument commonly given in opposition to physician-assisted suicide is the slippery slope argument. This is the fear that if physician assisted suicide is allowed in one situation, its use will gradually expand to include many situations that would never have been initially acceptable to society. Ethics experts Tom L. Beauchamp and James F. Childress explain: "Opponents of the legalization of physician-assisted dying have generally maintained that the practice inevitably would be expanded to include euthanasia, that the quality of palliative [relief of symptoms such as pain] care for all patients would deteriorate, that patients would be manipulated or coerced into requesting assistance in hastening death, that patients whose judgment was impaired would be allowed to request such assistance."[46]

> **Many people believe that instead of legalizing physician-assisted suicide for the terminally ill, palliative care should be improved.**

Critics argue that no evidence supports this theory. For example, in a 2007 report in the *Journal of Medical Ethics*, researchers analyzed data from Oregon and the Netherlands, looking at 10 different vulnerable groups of people including the elderly, the uninsured, and those with a low education level. In all the groups except AIDS patients, they found no evidence that people died more often as a result of physician-assisted suicide. The researchers conclude that there is "no current factual support for so-called slippery-slope concerns about the risks of legalization of assisted dying."[47]

End-of-Life Care

Many people believe that instead of legalizing physician-assisted suicide for the terminally ill, palliative care should be improved. They argue that many terminally ill people desire physician-assisted suicide only because they are not receiving adequate care. Critics insist that terminally ill patients are often in pain, afraid, or depressed, which motivates their desire to end their lives. Says palliative care specialist David Jeffrey, "Clinical experience shows that persistent requests for euthanasia or PAS [physician-assisted suicide] are infrequent if there is proper provision of palliative care."[48]

Yet others contend that even with good palliative care, a significant number of people will still desire physician-assisted suicide. In 2010 researchers Courtney S. Campbell and Jessica C. Cox revealed the results of an examination of more than ten years of data on terminally ill patients who ended their lives under Oregon's Death with Dignity Law. They report that between 1998 and 2009, 88.2 percent of terminally ill patients who used the state's Death with Dignity Law

> " It is often argued that legalization of physician-assisted suicide will threaten the relationship between patient and doctor. "

to end their lives were enrolled in hospice care, and conclude, "Terminally ill patients seeking physician-assisted death are receiving high-quality palliative care."[49] According to Nancy Berlinger of the Hastings Center, "It strongly suggests that the patients' reasons for using physician-assisted suicide were *unrelated* to their access to palliative care."[50]

Relationship with Doctors

It is often argued that legalization of physician-assisted suicide will threaten the relationship between patient and doctor, a relationship in which the doctor has traditionally been in the role of healing the patient, not ending his or her life. Thomas A. Shannon and Nicholas J. Kockler ask, "Will physician-assisted suicide infuse new—and some say inappropriate—goals (i.e., assistance in causing death) with more traditional goals (e.g., healing, curing, and preventing disease) in the practice of medicine?"[51] In its Code of Medical Ethics, the American Medical Association agrees, stating, "Physician-assisted suicide is fundamentally incompatible with the physician's role as healer."[52] The association sees physician-assisted suicide as abandonment of the patient and argues that instead, a physician should continue to care for the patient until the end of his or her life.

Others disagree, maintaining that physician-assisted suicide is not necessarily inconsistent with the physician's role. The World Federation of Right to Die Societies argues,

> The function of medicine is not only to sustain biological life but to relieve suffering. The question to be asked is whether a physician is causing more harm by favoring a slow agonizing death for a patient over one that is rapid and gentle. Allowing a patient to suffer when such suffering can only be alleviated by death, when the patient wants suffering to end whatever the cost, arguably is "doing harm."[53]

Legalization Experience in Oregon

While physician-assisted suicide is illegal in most places, it is legal in Oregon and Washington in the United States and in the countries of Switzerland and the Netherlands. Each place has different regulations about how physician-assisted suicide can legally take place. In Oregon, for example, a terminally ill patient can get a prescription for lethal drugs from his or her physician and self-administer them if certain conditions are met: He or she must be an adult, a resident of Oregon, capable of making health care decisions, and diagnosed with a terminal illness that will lead to death within six months. The diagnosis must be made by two doctors, and the terminally ill patient must make two oral requests at least 15 days apart, and a written request, for physician-assisted suicide.

> **Another way doctors can help patients die is to allow them to forgo or withdraw certain medical treatments that they need to live.**

In Oregon, as in other places where physician-assisted suicide is legal, various researchers and analysts use evidence to support both the opinion that legalization is harmful and that it is beneficial. Proponents maintain that legalization is working, with a relatively small number of people using it and no evidence of abuse. In an examination of the experience of the first 10 years in Oregon Campbell finds that

Death with dignity is the death of choice for relatively few persons. Before the act was implemented, opponents anticipated a demographic migration of near-terminal patients to Oregon, such that Oregon would become a "suicide center" for the terminally ill, with all sorts of ensuing social catastrophes. The empirical evidence does not bear out these projections. In ten years, 541 Oregon residents have received lethal prescriptions to end their lives; of this number, 341 patients actually ingested the drugs. These figures are not only lower than the substantial numbers predicted by opponents, they are even smaller than the more conservative estimates anticipated by advocates.[54]

Critics argue that physician-assisted suicide is underreported and that evidence of harm does exist, but the public is unaware of it. Rita L. Marker, executive director of the International Task Force on Euthanasia and Assisted Suicide, says,

The actual number could be far greater. From the time the law went into effect, Oregon officials in charge of formulating annual reports have conceded that "there's no way to know if additional deaths went unreported" because those officials have "no regulatory authority or resources to ensure compliance with the law." Equally unreliable are the statistics indicating that there have been no abuses or complications. The state has to rely on the word of doctors who prescribe the lethal drugs for such information.[55]

Forgoing or Withdrawing Treatment

In addition to assisted suicide, another way doctors can help patients die is to allow them to forgo or withdraw certain medical treatments that they need to live. For example, a doctor might turn off a mechanical respirator being used to keep alive somebody with severe brain damage. The famous case of Terri Schiavo illustrates some of the ethical debates involved with forgoing or withdrawing treatment. In 1995 Schiavo suffered from a heart attack, and due to a lack of oxygen to her brain she entered a vegetative state, where she was unresponsive and kept alive by a feeding tube. In 1998 her husband, Michael Schiavo, requested that her feeding tube be removed and she be allowed to die, arguing that she would not want to be kept alive in such a condition. Her parents disagreed, insisting that with treatment, she might recover. After a long court process and heated public debate on the issue, her tube was finally removed and she died in March 2005. Many people claimed that withdrawing treatment—removing the feeding tube—was essentially killing her, and this was unethical. Others contended that Schiavo did not have any quality of life and that removing the tube allowed her to die peacefully.

The debate over whether doctors should be allowed to help patients die is one of the oldest in biomedical ethics. With recent technology allowing medical professionals to keep patients alive longer than ever before, this issue has become increasingly important. Critics continue to debate whether or not individuals and doctors should legally have the choice to participate in physician-assisted suicide.

Primary Source Quotes*

Should Doctors Be Allowed to Help Patients Die?

> **"Legalising physician-assisted suicide would ... [allow terminally ill and incurably suffering people] a release from suffering that the sufferers themselves earnestly desire and request; refusing them denies their autonomy, and is at least unkind and at worst cruel."**

—A.C. Grayling, "Allowing People to Arrange Their Death Is a Simple Act of Kindness," *Times*, March 2009. www.timesonline.co.uk.

Grayling is a professor of applied philosophy at Birkbeck, University of London.

> **"Suicide isn't a medical act, and assisted suicide has nothing to do with autonomy as understood in medical ethics. Autonomy is the right to refuse medical treatment, not the right to a non-medical act performed by a physician."**

—Michael Egnor, "Physician-Assisted Suicide and Autonomy," *Evolution News and Views*, July 20, 2009. www.evolutionnews.org.

Egnor is a neurosurgeon.

Bracketed quotes indicate conflicting positions.

* Editor's Note: While the definition of a primary source can be narrowly or broadly defined, for the purposes of Compact Research, a primary source consists of: 1) results of original research presented by an organization or researcher; 2) eyewitness accounts of events, personal experience, or work experience; 3) first-person editorials offering pundits' opinions; 4) government officials presenting political plans and/or policies; 5) representatives of organizations presenting testimony or policy.

Primary Source Quotes

❝To explore how care of the dying could be improved is a more ethical course than legislating for PAS [physician-assisted suicide].❞

—David Jeffrey, *Against Physician Assisted Suicide: A Palliative Care Perspective*. New York: Radcliffe, 2009, p. 105.

Jeffrey is a medical doctor and expert on palliative care and the ethics of end-of-life care.

❝Numerous studies have found, however, that even among patients receiving good end-of-life care, there is still a consistently non-negligible percentage who request PAS [physician-assisted suicide] or evince a wish to hasten death. . . . The availability of such care will not come close to eliminating requests for PAS altogether.❞

—Michael B. Gill, "Is the Legalization of Physician-Assisted Suicide Compatible with Good End-of-Life Care?" *Journal of Applied Philosophy*, vol. 26, no. 1, 2009. p. 28.

Gill teaches in the philosophy department at the University of Arizona.

❝Patients trust that the physicians' actions are in their best interest with the goal of protecting life. Physician-assisted suicide endangers this trust relationship.❞

—Carrie Gordon Earll, "Physician-Assisted Suicide and Euthanasia," *CitizenLink*, July 12, 2010. www.citizenlink.com.

Earll is a senior policy analyst for bioethics at CitizenLink, a family advocacy organization.

❝Had euthanasia or 'assisted suicide' been legal I would have missed the best years of my life. And no one would ever have known that the future held such good times.❞

—Alison Davis, "Personal Stories," *Care Not Killing*, August 18, 2009. www.carenotkilling.org.

Davis suffers from spina bifida and emphysema.

66What emerges from the experience in places that have legalized assisted suicide is a highly subjective decision-making calculus that is applied without independent scrutiny, and which is open to considerable abuse.99

—Jim McGaughney, "Legalize Assisted Suicide? Not So Fast," Office of Protection and Advocacy for Persons with Disabilities, June 10, 2010. www.ct.gov.

McGaughney is executive director of the Office of Protection and Advocacy for Persons with Disabilities, a Connecticut state agency.

66Most supporters claim that assisted suicide will be narrowly limited to people with terminal illness, but these so-called 'narrow' proposals, if enacted, can easily expand. . . . The example of the Netherlands demonstrates clearly that assisted suicide cannot be limited to a small, targeted group once Pandora's box is open.99

—Marilyn Golden and Tyler Zoanni, "Killing Us Softly: The Dangers of Legalizing Assisted Suicide," *Disability and Health Journal*, January 2010. www.disabilityandhealthjnl.com.

Golden is a policy analyst and Zoanni is a former research associate for the Disability Rights Education & Defense Fund.

66Nor can PAS [physician-assisted suicide] be said to be a slippery slope. Statistics from the last twelve years of implementation in Oregon show that the law is actually used rarely: only about thirty patients a year.99

—Alissa Wassung, "Physician Assistance in Dying: The Doctor's Changing Role," *Yale Journal of Medicine and Law*, October 5, 2010. www.yalemedlaw.com.

Wassung is codirector of the Bioethics Society at Yale University.

Facts and Illustrations

Should Doctors Be Allowed to Help Patients Die?

- In the first 10 months after Washington's Death with Dignity Act took effect **63 people** requested and received a **lethal dose of medication**, according to the state's health department.

- According to Oregon's public health department, among those people utilizing the state's Death with Dignity Act in 2009, **10.2 percent** cited concerns about inadequate pain control.

- In August/September 2010, *Medscape* asked over 10,000 physicians, "Are there situations in which physician-assisted suicide should be allowed?" Of the respondents, **45.8 percent** answered "Yes" and **40.7 percent** answered "No."

- The University of Washington School of Medicine reports that surveys of physicians in practice show that about **1 in 5** will receive a request for physician-assisted suicide.

- The Hastings Center estimates that end-of-life care consumes approximately **10 to 12 percent** of the annual health care budget in the United States.

- For 2009 the National Hospice and Palliative Care Organization estimates that approximately **41.6 percent** of all deaths in the United States were of people under the care of a hospice program.

Most States Prohibit Physician-Assisted Suicide

This map shows state laws regarding physician-assisted suicide. The practice is prohibited by law in the majority of states and legal only in Washington and Oregon. In 2011, a number of states were considering legislation either banning or legalizing the practice.

Legend:
- PAS is legal
- Law prohibiting PAS
- Pending legislation legalizing PAS
- Pending legislation prohibiting PAS
- No specific legislation either legalizing or prohibiting

Source: Brianna Walden, "State of Physician Assisted Suicide in the United States," *Family Research Council Blog*, March 7, 2011. www.frcblog.com.

- In a study reported in a 2011 issue of *BMC Medical Ethics*, researchers sent questionnaires to 1,000 doctors in England and Wales and found that **49 percent** of doctors oppose physician-assisted suicide and **39 percent** support it.

Few Die Under Oregon's Death with Dignity Act

According to data on Oregon's Death with Dignity Act, since the act was passed in 1998 there has been an overall increase in the number of people receiving lethal prescriptions and in the number of deaths. However, the total number of people dying under the act remains relatively small; 59 people in 2009. Every year, more people receive a lethal prescription than actually use it to die.

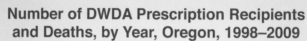

Number of DWDA Prescription Recipients and Deaths, by Year, Oregon, 1998–2009

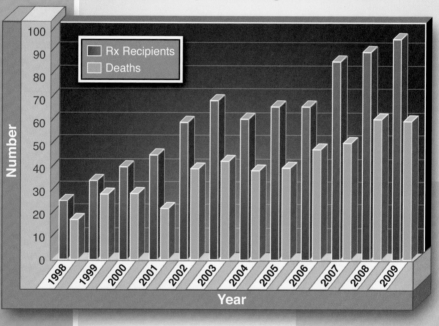

Source: Oregon Health Authority, "2009 Summary of Oregon's Death with Dignity Act," 2009. http://public.health.oregon.gov.

• The Hastings Center estimates that only **15 to 20 percent** of Americans have written advance directives that state their wishes regarding care such as life-sustaining medical treatment in case of a persistent vegetative state.

Dying Through Oregon's Death with Dignity Act

This chart reveals numerous characteristics of patients who have died under Oregon's Death with Dignity Act between 1998 and 2008. It shows that the majority are over age 65, are white, and are enrolled in hospice.

Characteristics	2009	1998–2008	Total
Sex			
Male (%)	31 (52.5)	213 (53.1)	244 (53.0)
Female (%)	28 (47.5)	188 (46.9)	216 (47.0)
Age			
18–34 (%)	2 (3.4)	4 (1.0)	6 (1.3)
35–44 (%)	1 (1.7)	11 (2.7)	12 (2.6)
45–54 (%)	2 (3.4)	32 (8.0)	34 (7.4)
55–64 (%)	9 (15.3)	85 (21.2)	94 (20.4)
65–74 (%)	13 (22.0)	114 (28.4)	127 (27.6)
75–84 (%)	24 (40.7)	112 (27.9)	136 (29.6)
85+ (%)	8 (13.6)	43 (10.7)	51 (11.1)
Education			
Less than high school (%)	3 (5.2)	30 (7.5)	33 (7.2)
High school graduate (%)	14 (24.1)	103 (25.7)	117 (25.5)
Some college (%)	13 (22.4)	92 (22.9)	105 (22.9)
Baccalaureate or higher (%)	28 (48.3)	176 (43.9)	204 (44.4)
Unknown	1	0	1
End-of-Life Care/Hospice			
Enrolled (%)	54 (91.5)	350 (87.7)	404 (88.2)
Not enrolled (%)	5 (8.5)	49 (12.3)	54 (11.8)
Unknown	0	2	2
End-of-Life Concerns			
Losing autonomy (%)	57 (96.6)	357 (89.9)	414 (90.8)
Less able to engage in activities making life enjoyable (%)	51 (86.4)	347 (87.4)	398 (87.3)
Loss of dignity (%)	54 (91.5)	228 (83.8)	282 (85.2)
Losing control of bodily functions (%)	31 (52.5)	233 (58.7)	264 (57.9)
Burden on family, friends/caregivers (%)	15 (25.4)	152 (38.3)	167 (36.6)
Inadequate pain control or concern about it (%)	6 (10.2)	95 (23.9)	101 (22.1)
Financial implications of treatment (%)	1 (1.7)	11 (2.8)	12 (2.6)

Source: Oregon Health Authority, "2009 Summary of Oregon's Death with Dignity Act," 2009. http://public.health.oregon.gov.

Key People and Advocacy Groups

Tom L. Beauchamp: Beauchamp is a professor of philosophy and a senior research scholar at the Kennedy Institute of Ethics at Georgetown University. He cowrote the *Belmont Report* in 1978, and later *Principles in Bioethics*, the first major bioethics textbook in the United States.

Daniel Callahan: Callahan is senior research scholar and president emeritus of the Hastings Center. He has written about a wide range of bioethical issues.

Arthur Caplan: Caplan is one of the nation's best-known bioethicists and has written or edited more than 30 books on the subject. He is Emanuel and Robert Hart Professor of Bioethics and director of the Center for Bioethics at the University of Pennsylvania in Philadelphia.

Ezekiel J. Emanuel: Emanuel serves as a health care adviser to President Barack Obama. Before that he was head of the Department of Bioethics at the Clinical Center of the National Institutes of Health.

Ruth R. Faden: Faden is the Philip Franklin Wagley Professor of Biomedical Ethics and executive director of the Johns Hopkins Berman Institute of Bioethics at Johns Hopkins University. She is also a senior research scholar at the Kennedy Institute of Ethics, Georgetown University. She has served on several national advisory committees and commissions concerned with bioethical issues.

Hastings Center: The Hastings Center is a nonprofit bioethics research institute that was founded in 1969 to address ethical issues in health, medicine, and the environment.

Al Jonsen: Al Jonsen was one of the first professors to teach bioethics in a medical school. He is currently professor emeritus of ethics in medicine at the University of Washington.

Leon Kass: Kass is an expert on numerous bioethical issues including in vitro fertilization, genetic screening, and organ transplantation. He was chairman of the President's Council on Bioethics from 2001 to 2005.

Kennedy Institute of Ethics: Established at Georgetown University in 1971, the Kennedy Institute of Ethics offers education and discourse about bioethical issues and has a comprehensive bioethics library.

Jack Kevorkian: Controversial physician Kevorkian was a well-known supporter of physician-assisted suicide. He claimed to have assisted at least 130 people in ending their own lives.

Edmund Pellegrino: Pellegrino is a former chairman of the President's Council on Bioethics and a past director of the Kennedy Institute of Ethics. He is the author of over 575 publications.

Peter Singer: Peter Singer is a well-known Australian philosopher and has authored numerous books and articles about various bioethics issues. He is the Ira W. DeCamp Professor of Bioethics at Princeton University.

Chronology

1999
Eighteen-year-old Jessie Gelsinger, suffering from a rare liver disease, dies in a human gene therapy experiment at the University of Pennsylvania.

1932
The Tuskegee syphilis study begins and lasts until 1972. Researchers study the effects of untreated syphilis on 400 African American men, withholding available treatment.

1990
The United States launches the Human Genome Project, a $20 billion effort to map and sequence the human genome; the first human gene therapy clinical trial is conducted.

1969
The Hastings Center is founded to study ethical problems and is influential in aiding the development of bioethics as a discipline.

1930 **1965** **2000**

1947
The Nuremberg Code for research on human subjects is adopted after revelations of Nazi experiments on Jews and other prisoners during the Holocaust.

1978
Louise Brown, the world's first test-tube baby, is born.

1974
The National Commission for the Protection of Human Subjects of Biomedical and Behavioral Research is created. In 1978 it issues the *Belmont Report*, which explains the fundamental ethical principles that should guide human subjects research.

1994
Oregon's Death with Dignity Act is passed, the first law in American history permitting physician-assisted suicide.

1998
Human embryonic stem cells are isolated and cultured for the first time; Congress passes the Fertility Clinic Success Rate and Certification Act, one of the few laws explicitly regulating assisted reproductive technology.

2000

In the first reported case of its kind Molly Nash receives a cord blood transfusion from a sibling who was genetically selected to be a donor match for Molly.

2010

Researchers at the J. Craig Venter Institute announce a major breakthrough in synthetic biology with the creation of the first self-replicating synthetic bacteria.

2002

A child genetically preselected not to carry a gene for Alzheimer's disease is born to a 30-year-old woman who carries the genetic mutation causing the disease.

2005

After seven years of legal battles, Terri Schiavo, a woman in a vegetative coma, dies after her feeding tube is removed.

2000

2010

2003

The Human Genome Project is completed.

2007

Researchers create induced pluripotent stem cells, cells that have properties similar to embryonic stem cells but are derived from adult skin cells.

2008

Washington becomes the second US state to legalize physician-assisted suicide; the 2008 Genetic Information Nondiscrimination Act prohibits insurance companies or employers from discriminating against people on the basis of DNA information.

2001

President George W. Bush announces that federal funding for embryonic stem cell research will be limited to existing lines.

2009

President Barack Obama reverses Bush's 2001 order limiting embryonic stem cell research.

Related Organizations

American Association for the Advancement of Science (AAAS)

1200 New York Ave. NW
Washington, DC 20005
phone: (202) 326-6400
e-mail: webmaster@aaas.org • website: www.aaas.org

The American Association for the Advancement of Science is an international organization dedicated to advancing science, innovation, and engineering around the world. It publishes the journal *Science*, as well as many reports, books, and scientific newsletters.

American Society of Law, Medicine, and Ethics (ASLME)

765 Commonwealth Ave., Suite 1634
Boston, MA 02215
phone: (617) 262-4990 • fax: (617) 437-7596
website: www.aslme.org

ASLME is a nonprofit educational organization that aims to provide debate and critical thought on the ethics of issues including genetic testing and research, end-of-life decisions, and informed consent. It publishes the *Journal of Law, Medicine & Ethics* and the *American Journal of Law & Medicine*.

Biotechnology Industry Organization (BIO)

1201 Maryland Ave. SW, Suite 900
Washington, DC 20024
phone: (202) 962-9200 • fax: (202) 488-6301
e-mail: info@bio.org • website: www.bio.org

The Biotechnology Industry Organization advocates and provides business development for its members. Its goal is to foster biotechnology innovation.

Compassion & Choices

PO Box 101810
Denver, CO 80250
phone: (800) 247-7421 • fax: (866) 312-2690
website: www.compassionandchoices.org

Compassion & Choices believes that too many Americans are not sufficiently educated about their choices at the end of life and thus suffer needlessly or turn to violent ends. The organization works to educate health care workers, policy makers, and individuals, and to improve care and expand choice at the end of life.

Death with Dignity National Center

520 SW 6th Ave., Suite 1030
Portland, OR 97204
phone: (503) 228-4415 • fax: (503) 228-7454
website: www.deathwithdignity.org

The Death with Dignity National Center is a nonprofit organization that provides education, research, and support in order to help preserve and promote Oregon's Death with Dignity laws. Its website offers research reports and personal stories about assisted suicide.

Genetics and Public Policy Center

1717 Massachusetts Ave. NW, Suite 530
Washington, DC 20036
phone: (202) 663-5971 • fax: (202) 663-5992
website: www.dnapolicy.org

The Genetics and Public Policy Center at Johns Hopkins University works to help policy makers and the public understand and respond to issues related to genetics. It conducts public surveys and policy analysis of advances in human genetics and issues statements on the likely outcomes of these advances. Its website includes testimony and issue briefs.

Hastings Center

21 Malcolm Gordon Rd.
Garrison, NY 10524
phone: (845) 424-4040
website: www.thehastingscenter.org

The Hastings Center, founded in 1969, is a nonpartisan, nonprofit bioethics research institute. Its researchers address ethical issues in health, medicine, and the environment. Its website includes reports on numerous bioethics issues including stem cell research, reproductive technology, and assisted suicide.

Kennedy Institute of Ethics

Healy Hall, 4th Floor, Georgetown University
Washington, DC 20057
phone: (202) 687-8099
e-mail: kicourse@georgetown.edu
website: http://kennedyinstitute.georgetown.edu

The Kennedy Institute of Ethics at Georgetown University was established in 1971 and aims to promote discussion of bioethical issues. It publishes the *Kennedy Institute of Ethics Journal*, and its website has a large research library.

National Human Genome Research Institute (NHGRI)

National Institutes of Health, Bldg. 31, Room 4B09
31 Center Dr., MSC 2152
9000 Rockville Pike
Bethesda, MD 20892-2152
phone: (301) 402-0911 • fax: (301) 402-2218
website: www.genome.gov

The National Human Genome Research Institute works to understand the structure and function of the human genome and the way it is related to health and disease. It supports the development of technology that will accelerate genome research. Its research includes study of the ethical implications of genome research.

National Library of Medicine (NLM)

8600 Rockville Pike
Bethesda, MD 20894
phone: (888) 346-3656 • fax: (301) 402-1384
website: www.nlm.nih.gov

The National Library of Medicine is the world's largest medical library. It provides information about all areas of biomedicine and health care.

For Further Research

Books

Tom L. Beauchamp and James F. Childress, *Principles of Biomedical Ethics*. New York: Oxford University Press, 2009.

Robert P. George and Christopher Tollefsen, *Embryo: A Defense of Human Life*. New York: Doubleday, 2008.

Joseph Panno, *Stem Cell Research*. New York: Facts On File, 2010.

Thomas A. Shannon and Nicholas J. Kockler, *An Introduction to Bioethics*. New York: Paulist, 2009.

Lewis Vaughn, *Bioethics: Principles, Issues, and Cases*. New York: Oxford University Press, 2010.

Robert M. Veatch, Amy M. Haddad, and Dan C. English, *Case Studies in Biomedical Ethics*. New York: Oxford University Press, 2010.

Doris Teichler Zallen, *To Test or Not to Test: A Guide to Genetic Screening and Risk*. Piscataway, NJ: Rutgers University Press, 2008.

Periodicals

David Biello, "Creation of Life," *Scientific American*, June 2010.

Courtney S. Campbell, "Ten Years of 'Death with Dignity,'" *New Atlantis*, Fall 2008.

Marcia Clemmitt, "Reproductive Ethics," *CQ Researcher*, May 15, 2009.

Allison Clemmons, "Organ Transplantation: Is the Best Approach a Legalized Market or Altruism?" *Journal of Healthcare Management*, July/August 2009.

Maura C. Flannery, "Mimicking Nature, or at Least Trying To," *American Biology Teacher*, September 2010.

A.C. Grayling, "Allowing People to Arrange Their Death Is a Simple Act of Kindness," *Times*, March 2009.

Ronald M. Green, "Building Baby from the Genes Up," *Washington Post*, April 13, 2008.

David Lemberg, "Distributive Justice and Assisted Reproductive Technology," *Bioethics—Global, National, Local*, June 23, 2010.

New Scientist, "Still the Gold Standard: Halting Embryonic Stem Cell Research Now Would Be Nothing Short of Rash," May 3, 2008.

Christiane Nusslein-Volhard, "Manipulating the Human Embryo," *USA Today*, January 2011.

Ramesh Ponnuru, "Out of the Freezer," *National Review*, April 6, 2009.

Sandroff Ronni, "Direct-to-Consumer Genetic Tests and the Right to Know," *Hastings Center Report*, September/October 2010.

Scientific American, "Designing Rules for Designer Babies," May 2009.

Elizabeth Svoboda, "The Essential Guide to Stem Cells: Everything You Need to Know About the Hottest Topic in Medicine, from Big-league Breakthroughs and New Therapies to Emerging Health Risks and the Patients Willing to Take Them," *Popular Science*, June 2009.

Internet Sources

American Medical Association, "AMA's Code of Medical Ethics: Principles, Opinions, and Reports," n.d. www.ama-assn.org/ama/pub/physician-resources/medical-ethics/code-medical-ethics.shtml.

Coalition for the Advancement of Medical Research, "A Catalyst for Cures: Embryonic Stem Cell Research," January 12, 2009. www.camradvocacy.org/resources/camr_wp.pdf.

Gregory Kutz, "Direct-to-Consumer Genetic Tests: Misleading Test Results Are Further Complicated by Deceptive Marketing and Other Questionable Practices," testimony before the Subcommittee on Oversight and Investigations, Committee on Energy and Commerce, House of Representatives, June 22, 2010. www.gao.gov/new.items/d10847t.pdf.

National Commission for the Protection of Human Subjects of Biomedical and Behavioral Research, *Belmont Report: Ethical Principles and Guidelines for the Protection of Human Subjects of Research*, Department of Health, Education, and Welfare, April 18, 1979. www.nmmu.ac.za/documents/rcd/The%20Belmont%20Report.pdf.

National Institutes of Health, "Handbook: Help Me Understand Genetics: Genetic Testing," February 13, 2011. http://ghr.nlm.nih.gov/handbook/testing.pdf.

———, "Stem Cell Basics." http://stemcells.nih.gov/staticresources/info/basics/SCprimer2009.pdf.

Source Notes

Overview

1. Robert M. Veatch, Amy M. Haddad, and Dan C. English, *Case Studies in Biomedical Ethics*. New York: Oxford University Press, 2010, p. xxi.
2. Lewis Vaughn, *Bioethics: Principles, Issues, and Cases*. New York: Oxford University Press, 2010, pp. 51–52.
3. Ronald M. Green, "Building Baby from the Genes Up," *Washington Post*, April 13, 2008. www.washingtonpost.com.
4. National Institutes of Health, "Stem Cells and Diseases," August 19, 2010. http://stemcells.nih.gov.
5. National Institutes of Health, "Stem Cells and Diseases."
6. Vaughn, *Bioethics*, p. 354.
7. Presidential Commission for the Study of Bioethical Issues, "New Directions: The Ethics of Synthetic Biology and Emerging Technologies," December 2010. www.bioethics.gov.
8. Thomas A. Shannon and Nicholas J. Kockler, *An Introduction to Bioethics*. New York: Paulist, 2009, p. 290.
9. Tuskegee University, "Research Ethics: The Tuskegee Syphilis Study." www.tuskegee.edu.
10. Arthur Caplan, "The Ethical Good of the 'Yes' Option," in *New York Times*, "Should Laws Push for Organ Donation?" May 2, 2010. www.nytimes.com.
11. Presidential Commission for the Study of Bioethical Issues, "New Directions."
12. Shannon and Kockler, *An Introduction to Bioethics*, p. 5.

Can Genetic Testing and Manipulation Be Done Ethically?

13. Arthur Caplan, "Disability-Free World May Not Be a Better Place," MSNBC.
com, February 18, 2010. www.msnbc.msn.com.
14. Doris Teichler Zallen, *To Test or Not to Test: A Guide to Genetic Screening and Risk*. Piscataway, NJ: Rutgers University Press, 2008, p. 2.
15. 23andMe, "About23andMe: Policy Forum." www.23andme.com.
16. Gregory Kutz, "Direct-to-Consumer Genetic Tests: Misleading Test Results Are Further Complicated by Deceptive Marketing and Other Questionable Practices," testimony before the Subcommittee on Oversight and Investigations, Committee on Energy and Commerce, House of Representatives, June 22, 2010. www.gao.gov.
17. National Human Genome Research Institute, "Genetic Information Nondiscrimination Act of 2008," September 28, 2010. www.genome.gov.
18. US National Library of Medicine, "What Is Gene Therapy?" *Handbook: Help Me Understand Genetics*, January 9, 2011. http://ghr.nlm.nih.gov.
19. Shannon and Kockler, *An Introduction to Bioethics*, p. 244.
20. Richard Hayes, "Genetically Modified Humans? No Thanks," *Washington Post*, April 15, 2008. www.washingtonpost.com.
21. American Medical Association, "Code of Medical Ethics: Principles of Medical Ethics: Opinion 2.11—Gene Therapy." www.ama-assn.org.

Is the Use of Human Embryos in Stem Cell Research Ethical?

22. Christopher Reeve, "Federal Funding for Stem Cell Research," testimony before the Subcommittee on Labor, Health and Human Services, and Ed-

ucation, and Related Agencies, Committee on Appropriations, April 26, 2000. www.chrisreevehomepage.com.

23. United States Conference of Catholic Bishops, "On Embryonic Stem Cell Research," June 2008. www.usccb.org.

24. Reeve, "Federal Funding for Stem Cell Research."

25. United States Conference of Catholic Bishops, "On Embryonic Stem Cell Research."

26. White House, "White House Fact Sheet: Embryonic Stem Cell Research," August 9, 2001. www.whitehouse.gov.

27. University of Minnesota Stem Cell Institute, "Q & A on Embryonic Stem Cell Research," September 16, 2009. www.stemcell.umn.edu.

28. Harvard Stem Cell Institute, "Frequently Asked Questions." www.hsci.harvard.edu.

29. Center for Bioethics & Human Dignity, "An Overview of Stem Cell Research." www.cbhd.org.

30. American Association for the Advancement of Science, "American Association for the Advancement of Science (AAAS) Statement Regarding the President's Veto of the Stem Cell Research Enhancement Act and the New Executive Order," June 20, 2007. www.aaas.org.

31. Francis S. Collins, testimony before the Senate Subcommittee on Labor—HHS—Education Appropriations, September 16, 2010. www.nih.gov.

32. Harvard Stem Cell Institute, "Frequently Asked Questions."

33. Joseph Panno, *Stem Cell Research*. New York: Facts On File, 2010, p. 87.

Is Assisted Reproductive Technology Ethical?

34. Timothy F. Murphy, "The Ethics of Helping Transgender Men and Women Have Children," *Perspectives in Biology and Medicine*, Winter 2010, p. 57.

35. Ethics Committee of the American Society for Reproductive Medicine, "Access to Fertility Treatment by Gays, Lesbians, and Unmarried Persons," *ASRM Committee Reports*, October 2009, p. 1,192.

36. Michael J. Sandel, *The Case Against Perfection: Ethics in the Age of Genetic Engineering*. London: Belknap Press of Harvard University Press, 2007, p. 45.

37. James Hughes, "What Are Reproductive Rights?" *Institute for Ethics and Emerging Technologies*, August 13, 2010. http://ieet.org.

38. Vaughn, *Bioethics*, p. 359.

39. Quoted in Gina Kolata, "Picture Emerging on Genetic Risks of IVF," *New York Times*, February 16, 2009. www.nytimes.com.

40. David Lemberg, "Distributive Justice and Assisted Reproductive Technology," *Bioethics—Global, National, Local*, June 23, 2010. http://davidlemberg.com.

41. Arthur Caplan, "Ethics and Fees," in "The Baby Market," *New York Times*, December 29, 2009. www.nytimes.com.

42. Quoted in Abigail Haworth, "Surrogate Mothers: Womb for Rent," *Marie Claire*, July 16, 2009. www.marieclaire.com.

Should Doctors Be Allowed to Help Patients Die?

43. Quoted in Associated Press, "Physician-Assisted Suicide Advocate Dr. Jack Kevorkian to Be Released from Prison," *Fox News*, May 27, 2007. www.foxnews.com.

44. Comment on "Death with Dignity Is a Life Choice," *Death with Dignity National Center*, January 27, 2011.

www.deathwithdignity.org.

45. Michael Egnor, "Physician-Assisted Suicide and Autonomy," *Evolution News and Views*, July 20, 2009. www.evolutionnews.org.

46. Tom L. Beauchamp and James F. Childress, *Principles of Biomedical Ethics*. New York: Oxford University Press, 2009, p. 178.

47. Margaret P. Battin et al., "Legal Physician-Assisted Dying in Oregon and the Netherlands: Evidence Concerning the Impact on Patients in 'Vulnerable' Groups," *Journal of Medical Ethics*, vol. 33. 2007, http://jme.bmj.com.

48. David Jeffrey, *Against Physician Assisted Suicide: A Palliative Care Perspective*. New York: Radcliffe, 2009, p. 50.

49. Courtney S. Campbell and Jessica C. Cox, "Hospice and Physician-Assisted Death: Collaboration, Compliance, and Complicity," *Hastings Center Report*, September/October 2010. www.thehastingscenter.org.

50. Quoted in Wayne J. Guglielmo, "Exclusive Ethics Survey: 'Doctor, Will You Help Me Die?'" *Medscape Medical Ethics*, November 23, 2010. www.medscape.com.

51. Shannon and Kockler, *An Introduction to Bioethics*, p. 194.

52. American Medical Association, "Code of Medical Ethics: Principles of Medical Ethics: Opinion 2.211—Physician-Assisted Suicide." www.ama-assn.org.

53. World Federation of Right to Die Societies, "Questions and Answers: Doesn't Assisted Dying Violate Medical Tradition?" www.worldrtd.net.

54. Courtney S. Campbell, "Ten Years of 'Death with Dignity,'" *New Atlantis*, Fall 2008. www.thenewatlantis.com.

55. Rita L. Marker, "Correspondence: Debating 'Death with Dignity,'" *New Atlantis*, Winter 2009.

List of Illustrations

Index

Note: Boldface page numbers indicate illustrations.

About the Author

Andrea C. Nakaya, a native of New Zealand, holds a BA in English and an MA in communications from San Diego State University. She currently lives in Encinitas, California, with her husband and their two children.